CW00323459

ARE YOU EXPECTING TOO MUCH

FROM YOUR CHILD?

ARE YOU EXPECTING TOO MUCH
FROM YOUR CHILD?

Dr Fiona Subtosky

Piccadilly Press • London

Phototypeset from author's disk
Printed and bound by Biddles Ltd., Guildford
for the publishers, Piccadilly Press Ltd.,
5 Castle Road, London NW1 8PR

A catalogue record for this book is available
from the British Library

ISBN: 1 85340 261 3

Dr Fiona Subotsky lives in South London. She has two grown-up sons. She
has worked as a consultant child psychiatrist for many years, and works at
the Maudsley and King's College Hospital in London. She has written a
number of papers on aspects of child psychiatry and has co-authored a book
Does My Child Need Help. This is her first book for
Piccadilly Press.

CONTENTS

INTRODUCTION

"The joys of parents are secret, and so are their griefs and fears."
Francis Bacon

"A wise son maketh a glad father: but a foolish son is the heaviness of his mother."
Psalms

When you expect too much from your child, you are bound to be disappointed. Under "disappointment" the thesaurus offers as similar words and ideas – regret, tantalisation, frustration, bafflement, disillusion, let-down, humiliation, and failure.

All of these negative emotions are a daily experience, usually in a trivial kind of way – for instance the car will not start, the mail-order sweater is slightly the wrong colour.

The essential precursors are: hope and expectation.

Whether embarked upon intentionally or unintentionally, the arrival of a child is looked forward to with the greatest of hope and expectation. This is reflected in Western Judaeo-Christian culture with the focus on the Messiah – the perfect child that is to come and save all. The nine months' period of invisible development is a time of speculation. There is, at the very least, guessing and wishing about the sex of the baby:

"I guess it will be a boy – it kicks so much."

"I think this time it's a girl – the lie is different."

And especially – "Will the baby be normal and healthy? How can we cope if it isn't?"

Some of this guesswork has now been reduced by modern technology – the intra-uterine scan, and a variety of tests for abnormalities. But it is not clear how much this has reduced anxieties – or simply altered them. For instance, while I was working at an intensive care baby unit, there were cases where scans revealed the death of a twin – a loss which previously might have remained unknown. This is a kind of retrospective disappointment. Generally, however, it is helpful to have advance warning of difficulties, to begin to prepare for them.

It is not a new criticism of antenatal preparation to say that it concentrates on the pregnancy and the experience of childbirth, and the immediate arrangements that are necessary for a new baby, without laying a foundation of what to expect next. In these days of small families, not only are a much higher proportion of births "firsts" for the parents, but they are likely to have had no direct experience of looking after babies at all. This is another reason why the baby needs to be "right first time". We now expect our babies to be well and to survive, and we are mostly correct.

According to Philippe Aries, in his book *Centuries of Childhood*, "The general feeling was, and for a long time remained, that one had several children in order to keep a few." So, in the past, perhaps there was more sadness but less disappointment for parents as expectations were necessarily lower.

Sometimes hopes and wishes are quite explicit:

"We would really like a boy, but of course we'll love whatever comes."

" I do hope this baby is easier than the one before."

" I do hope this baby has not got the disease that runs in the family."

But often, thoughts about the future child are not explicitly voiced or even consciously thought about. They may be obvious assumptions, such as of good health, or unconsidered expectations such as high intelligence. Sometimes the expectation is not so much of a property of the baby, but of the parental response, such as of "instant" love, and of a straightforward adaptation to the new roles of mothering and fathering. Sometimes the disappointed expectations only emerge as the child develops, and the reasons for the disappointed feelings and their strength may be far from clear. Often the feelings of dissatisfaction, irritation or disappointment are so strong that the parent knows that they are irrational, but this may simply add to their guilt rather than bring relief.

One particular child may become an especial focus or preoccupation. This can be positive in terms of intensive attention, although it may lead to over-protection and/or spoiling. However, the attention may be negative, even rejecting. Sometimes both positive and negative attention are combined.

As a child psychiatrist I mainly see families who are in the most extreme distress about their children. But even in normal, everyday family life, emotions are naturally intense, because people's closest relationships are within the family. As nothing can go perfectly always, there are bound to be feelings of disappointment from time to time, especially when expectations dear to the heart are not met.

As I began to research this book, and discussed the project with friends and acquaintances, I found that this concept of disappointment struck a chord with all the parents and the professionals working with families. I also realised that disappointment was often a basic theme for many of the worried families that I see. Yet there is very little written about it directly.

I start by considering briefly some of the theoretical frameworks which may be helpful in understanding the issues. Then I give examples of various situations in which parents are commonly disappointed, with case studies drawn from clinical practice. Most parents will recognise at least some of these situations, even though their own experiences may not be as extreme. Finally, I consider different ways in which parents might try to avoid and overcome the problems associated with high expectations and the resulting disappointment.

Of course, as with many difficulties, the first thing to realise is that you are not alone in what you experience.

THEORETICAL FRAMEWORKS

"Before I got married I had six theories about bringing up children; now I have six children and no theories."
  Lord Rochester

In the first place, ideas usually arise from observation and are tested later. My observations on parents and their disappointed expectations are only first thoughts, not a scientific study. But even at this stage, various theoretical approaches can help shed light on the causes of parental disappointment, and they may sometimes offer a way forward.

COGNITIVE APPROACHES

"Cognitive therapy" is now accepted as a successful method of intervention by many psychologists and psychiatrists. Its basic tenets, however, are not very new, and indeed the common-sense and reasoning approach has been part of the focus of practical philosophers from ancient times.

1. IFD DISEASE

Wendell Johnson, an American psychologist writing in the 1940s, introduced a very relevant concept which deserves to be more widely known – "IFD Disease". This stands for: "from Idealisation to Frustration to Demoralisation", which Johnson termed "the basic design of our common maladjustment". He approached people's problems by trying to find out the way they evaluated things – their ideals, goals, beliefs, assumptions, attitudes, conflicts, fears and resentments. These "evaluations" were mainly verbal, and were often unclearly expressed. They arise from family background, social culture, expressions of authority and so forth, and are more or less rationally based.

Wendell Johnson's form of treatment was to encourage the "students" (an explicitly educational and rational term) to express their problems in their own words. He then discussed with them the connections between their evaluations and behaviour and their irrational thinking. Without going into too much detail, these would include errors of thinking such as black/white either/or assumptions, and unrealistic goals.

An example of black and white thinking would be that if a child tells a lie he is viewed as completely bad; a child is seen as either totally good or totally bad with no "shades of grey". "Unrealistic goals" are obviously set by some parents for their children and can lead to anger and disappointment. When these attitudes are explored thoroughly by the "students", with some guidance, they begin to realise that they are illogical and try to amend them.

2. RATIONAL EMOTIVE THERAPY

Albert Ellis, from the 1960s on, repudiated the field of psychoanalysis in which he was trained and popularised a form of "rational psychotherapy" called Rational Emotive Therapy. RET emphasises the fact that "emotional disturbance nearly always involves an absolutistic *should*, *ought*, or *must* that disturbed people are consciously or unconsciously demanding of themselves, of others, or of the universe".

Ellis has another three-letter mnemonic – ABC theory. First, there is an Activating Experience (sometimes also referred to as an Adversity) – that is, something occurs, for instance you get fired from your job. The Consequence is that you feel depressed and stop going out. In between there must be a Belief, or attitude about it that you tell yourself, such as – "Anyone who loses their job must be no good."

The basic premise is that people do not directly react emotionally or behaviourally to the events they encounter in their lives; rather, people cause their own reactions by the way they interpret the events they experience.

Ellis's suggestion is to search for the irrational shoulds and musts, and also the unrealistically-based beliefs. Very commonly these are "all-or-nothing" beliefs, or ones not based soundly on facts.

3

3. COGNITIVE THERAPY

Aaron Beck was originally a psychoanalyst who, using the standard procedure of free association, encouraged his patients to air their ideas freely. He discovered that there was often an accompanying self-critical commentary, more obvious in some patients than others. These "automatic thoughts" seemed rapid and fleeting. They usually preceded a negative emotion such as fear or depression. He also found that, with some people, their criticisms took a visual form, so that for instance, a depressive might always have a mental image of himself failing at a task. He also recommends a systematic approach for a client in therapy whereby they note their negative thoughts and attempt to interrupt or oppose them.

4. OPTIMISTS AND PESSIMISTS

The concept of "Learned Helplessness" was first proposed by the psychologist Martin Seligman. He noted many experiments which showed that animals repeatedly exposed to an unpleasant situation from which they cannot escape will tend to do nothing at all when put in a similar situation – even when they could now easily escape. Human subjects sometimes behaved in a similar "helpless" way – but were sometimes much more persistent. Seligman started to look at this in terms of "explanatory style", using the models of the cognitive theorists described above.

He found that "optimists" characteristically evaluated negative events as unique instances and probably someone else's fault. On the other hand they interpreted positive events as normal and due to their own good fortune or ability. "Pessimists" by contrast, evaluated negative events as being normal, and their own fault; they evaluated positive events as "one-offs" and due to chance rather than their own contribution. In *Winnie-the-Pooh*, Eeyore is a characteristic extreme pessimist, while the bouncy Tigger is of course an optimist.

What you perceive about a situation therefore depends on how you perceive it. You may have a characteristic way of doing this, based on experience or upbringing which didn't always bring you the greatest happiness or the best possible outcome. Interestingly, pessimists, given training and encouragement, can become much more optimistic – they are not temperamentally as doomed as they may think. Even Eeyore managed to see the good side of his strange birthday presents from Pooh and Piglet – an empty honey jar and a broken balloon!

5. COGNITIVE DISSONANCE

Leo Festinger's theory of "Cognitive Dissonance" was that, if two perceptions or beliefs held by a person seem to oppose each other, the person tends to want to reduce the tension by changing one or both of them. An example of this is the "sour grapes" story in Aesop's Fables. The fox sees some grapes and tries to get them. However, he cannot reach them, and so says to himself "I'm sure they were sour anyway."

This response to a disappointment is a way of reducing the chance of regret. However, this kind of behaviour may not necessarily be in the person's best interests or lead to greater happiness. The fox might have found another way to get the grapes, for instance, if he had considered altering his own actions rather than blaming the grapes – but this would have taken a bit more effort.

An example of this with parents might be: "I have done everything I can as a parent. Therefore if I can't get my child to behave it must be because he was born useless like his Uncle Jack."

PSYCHODYNAMIC IDEAS

1. DEFENCE MECHANISMS

People may have "faulty thoughts" but why and how do they arise? Psychodynamic ideas are sometimes put in opposition to cognitive-behavioural approaches, but are attempting to cast light on a different area. One of Sigmund Freud's ideas, elaborated later by his daughter, Anna Freud, was the psychological concept of "defence mechanisms". When other more rational approaches may not be available "The ego makes use of various methods of fulfilling its task ... of avoiding danger, anxiety and unpleasantness." Painful ideas are thus put out of consciousness or displaced or disguised.

Sigmund Freud distinguished between the *idea* and the

effect (or emotion) attached to it. And so "Denial" is the correct word for the hiding of a thought, and "Repression" for the concealment of the associated emotions.

If someone has undergone a painful bereavement, it could be "denial" if they never mention it. Alternatively, they may be able to discuss their loss with total rationality and lack of emotion; this could be an example of "repression" – especially if the unhappy emotion appears at other times or attached to other issues. These mechanisms are usually assumed to be unconscious, yet people can often be at least partially aware that they are trying to spare themselves distress, saying for instance, "I don't want to talk about that – it is just too painful." And such mechanisms are not just a function of the individual, they may be evident in a family, where by common consent it seems that some things – like a deserting father – are never referred to.

The concept of "Projection" is that "an internal perception is suppressed, and instead its content, after undergoing a certain degree of distortion, enters consciousness in the form of an external perception". An example commonly given is that person A hates person B and has even done him some injury. Person A, however, says person B hates him and has offended him. Person A then feels justified in his retaliation. This sort of process is even more obvious if you substitute the word "country" for "person". In some of the case histories given later, one can perceive this kind of process between parent and child.

All of these processes are very natural and usual; however,

they can cause considerable distortion in the way a child's behaviour is viewed and evaluated.

2. ATTACHMENT AND BONDING

In the 1940s, observations of motherless babies and young children in institutions led to considerations of attachment in humans and how this might be important for later adjustment. John Bowlby in particular developed these ideas and described them in his influential book *Attachment and Loss*. Interest began to focus on the very early experiences of babies and their mothers. Was it good for human new-borns to be removed instantly from their mothers? Perhaps it was essential that they should be with their natural mothers at all times and that any form of separation was harmful. Did any separation interfere with "attachment" and the later personality development of the child? Did lack of "bonding" prevent the mother caring for her child – did she too have some sort of sensitive period for forming affectionate bonds? (In this context, a "bond" is a tie from parent to infant, whereas the word "attachment" refers to the tie in the opposite direction, from infant to parent.)

This trend of thought had mostly good effects on the care of new-borns. Nowadays babies are much more likely to be given to their mothers as soon as possible after birth, and the mother is, wherever possible, encouraged to care for her baby, even if it is quite tiny or unwell. Awareness of this has spread widely. Some parents do say they are less "well-bonded" to one child than another and that they cannot feel love for them. They may put this feeling down to a series of adverse experiences in the neonatal period, as will be seen in some of the case histories that follow.

The quality of an infant's attachment to its mother has been studied using the "Stranger Situation" test – in which a young child is observed first with its mother, then as a stranger enters, then as the mother leaves and later returns. Among American babies at least, there does seem to be a characteristic pattern of response associated with more responsive parenting. The child is content to explore when its mother is present, and will go, or reach out, to her when she returns. Children from disadvantaged families are more likely to reject, be angry with, or avoid their mothers.

However, there are also differences between cultures – which may reflect what is normal in, say, Germany or Japan. In addition, it has been pointed out that from an evolutionary point of view, it is not necessarily most effective for a mother to give very close attention to one child – there may be other children who need her. It is therefore equally possible that a baby may be "programmed" to cope with a variety of levels and types of attention from mothers.

3. THE GOOD ENOUGH MOTHER
Donald Winnicott, a psychoanalyst and paediatrician, turned the problem on its head. His concept of the "good enough mother" implies that it would not be helpful for

the child if the parent met all its needs, and protected it from all disappointment. In fact, it is essential that the parent "fails" the child in small ways. Children need to understand that they are separate beings so they can start to meet some of their own needs instead of always relying on other people. He called this the mother's "job of disillusioning", and it is difficult for both the mother and the baby.

2

NATURE OR NURTURE?

"Nature is more powerful than education."
  Benjamin Disraeli

"The tender youth of a child is like the tempering of new wax, apt to receive any form."
  John Lyly

"Give me a dozen healthy infants, well formed, and my own specified world to bring them up in, and I will guarantee to take any one at random and train him to become any type of specialist I might select – doctor, lawyer, artist, merchant chief, and yes, even beggarman and thief, regardless of his talents, penchants, tendencies, abilities, vocations, and the race of his ancestors."
  J.B. Watson

As can be seen from the quotations above, whether a child's character and achievements are mainly the product of its genes or its environment has been a source of continued debate. "Nature" is understood to be the physical and psychological characteristics we are born with, and

"Nurture" is what happens later due to the environment. It is now becoming clearer that there can also be genetically programmed developments after birth, which is not surprising as one considers the obvious developmental stages of childhood and beyond.

Before we look at some of the currently known facts, let us continue with the irrational components of human thinking and consider why and how, when under stress, a parent may choose one theory rather than another to try to account for their offspring's failure to live up to their hopes.

THE PARENT'S THEORY TABLE

	NATURE	NURTURE
SELF	Like me	I did it
OTHER PARENT	Like him/her	He/she did it
CHILD	Born evil	Got him/herself into trouble
OTHER EVENT	Something happened before or during birth	Something happened after birth

SELF/NATURE

Starting with the Self/Nature cell: the parent accepts that the child's fault or weakness resembles characteristics of themselves, or of their own family. If this makes the parent feel guilty, they may prefer another sort of explanation. Alternatively, the parent may explicitly identify with the "fault" – as in "I was always shy like that," or "I used to truant myself" – with the usual implication that this could fit in with their expectations and so, maybe, sympathy rather than correction is called for.

OTHER PARENT/NATURE

With the "Other Parent/Nature" type, the "blame" lies away from the self and with the other parent or their family's "heredity". This may be an easy option, especially if the blamed parent is absent. This kind of explanation is seen in some of the cases discussed later where the child is coming in for heavy criticism. Adoption can be a situation where this sort of theory is often considered.

CHILD/NATURE

The next type of explanation, "Child/Nature", is not very fashionable in our present culture, at least not overtly. But you don't have to look very far to hear about "Original Sin", which implies that everyone is born wicked and has to bear responsibility for it from the start. And on a more individual basis, there is the idea of the "changeling" – a horrible child who is not one's own. That these ideas are still current is more apparent in horror films such as *Rosemary's Baby* and *The Omen*. A more constructive use of this type of explanation is when it is used as an excuse for a phase: "All two-year-olds have tantrums, don't they?" This is a non-disappointing, hopeful idea, with reduction of blame all round. It can be a useful suggestion for parents who may not have thought of this for themselves.

OTHER EVENT/NATURE

The "Other Event/Nature" type of explanation may be invoked when it is known or thought probable that, say, an infection occurred during the pregnancy, or the birth had a series of difficulties. Although the mother may feel guilty, often parents present this kind of history with much anger towards the medical system, which seems to have failed them.

NURTURE

Moving on to the "Nurture" column: a parent who thinks that his or her own actions may account for the child's misdeeds or faults, can feel very uncomfortable and guilty. This idea is frequently ascribed to (or "projected onto") people who are trying to help – "The therapist at Child Guidance made out it was all my fault." Parents with slightly different management techniques may try to get each other to accept the guilt, and are sometimes at least partially successful, as this may have the advantage of reducing interparental conflict.

OTHER PARENT/NURTURE

It is very common for a parent to blame the other parent for what they have done, or are doing. Both parents may be accusing each other – "She's too soft"/"No, he's too impatient." This kind of mutual attack can continue long after divorce.

CHILD/NURTURE

Although a very young child can hardly be held responsible for his or her own environment, the "Child/Nurture" type of explanation is used when, for instance, the parent blames the child for constantly choosing the "wrong kind of friend", or insisting on eating the "wrong kind of food".

OTHER EVENT/NURTURE

The "Other Event/Nurture" type of explanation is quite a comfortable one emotionally: that food additives are causing misbehaviour, or that a class teacher is picking on the child. I am not making any judgements about the likelihood of external factors contributing to the situation, only pointing out that it is quite a "face-saver" for a family in search of a reason. Frequently, a parent brings a child to the clinic and assumes that only the child "knows" what is causing the trouble, and we, the professionals, must take him or her away and find out what it is. In many such cases, the cause of distress is quite obvious. In others, the child is also committed to the "Don't know" school of thought!

TEMPERAMENT AND DEVELOPMENT

Babies are born with very different personalities, as mothers know. As they grow to toddlerhood this becomes even more marked. The possibility that a person's temperament is evident even when they are an infant was developed by Stella Chess and Alexander Thomas over many years. Temperament does not seem to be fixed – it will be affected by situation and time, but there are important continuities. It is now thought from twin studies that genes account for about half the variability seen in temperament.

Thus a baby may be born with a tendency to be more or less anxious or active, and its personality may either match or not match what the parent was hoping for and can best cope with. Similar personality characteristics may evoke different responses from different parents. This is particularly clear across cultures. For instance, a one-year-old baby who is still waking a lot at night may be the source of much family stress in a London or New York family, but no problem to a Japanese mother who has the child in her bed. The response to the child will then determine other aspects of its personality, showing what a truly interactive process this is.

The following interesting finding was reported by Thomas and Chess. Some Masai babies had been rated according to how difficult or not difficult they were. When the investigator returned after a period of great stress and famine, it was found that most of the "least difficult" babies had died, while all of the "most difficult" babies had survived. It seems that what may be undesirable characteristics to a parent may have survival value to the individual child.

And so, over the first few months, aspects of a child's personality unfold as part of normal development, from the first smile to the first distress at a stranger's face. The mother is rightly proud of all progress, even of the first tooth – towards which she has made less contribution than to many other aspects of development.

Blame and praise are given to the mother by others and also to the mother or father by themselves. Only too commonly, it is "Aren't you lucky?" for an easy baby, whereas for a difficult baby it is criticism or not-so-subtle suggestions that the mother should do things differently. In the first case, the happy result is assumed to be due entirely to the child's nature, and in the second case, entirely to the mother's nurture. Wouldn't it be pleasant for the reverse to occur – that the mother of a contented baby should be asked the secrets of her success and the mother of the difficult baby given lots of sympathy?

A baby looks the way it does partly because it has its father's nose and its mother's eyes, say, but overwhelmingly what it looks like and behaves like is a baby, and we know it will develop in a more or less predictable way into a much larger and more self-sufficient being – an adult – given the right circumstances. Nursery and school teachers can often take this more relaxed and detached approach, but then, they are not the people with the individual tie to the child.

CAN ENVIRONMENT MAKE A DIFFERENCE?
There is much evidence that a child's circumstances can affect adjustment and achievement. This affect is not as straightforward as was once thought; for instance, early negative experiences can often be considerably ameliorated by later positive ones. And some children seem more "resilient" than others and can do well despite major or long-term stresses.

There are many examples where early difficulties, whether of temperament or of illness, are not evident later if the circumstances are good. But they can combine with adverse circumstances such as rejection, maternal depression or poor family support to lead to a poor outcome for the child.

This is good news for our theme. Parents can and do make a difference, even to children who start off with disadvantages. And even if mistakes are made in the early years, not everything is fixed by fate, and changes can be made, both by parents and by later choices or circumstances of the growing child.

Can schools make a difference? There is plenty of evidence that they do. Nursery education can make an enduring difference, especially for disadvantaged children, as has been show by the follow-up of the Head-Start programme in the USA. It has also been shown that schools with certain characteristics, such as clear rules, rewards and so on, achieve better results than other schools with a similar intake. Even one good teacher can make a difference.

CAN PARENTS LEARN?

It is clear that parents can contribute to their children's maladjustment, by ineffective management, by being over-critical or punitive, or by general family discord. Can they learn to alter their behaviour to the benefit of children? Although the methods of measuring parental behaviour, childhood disturbance, and types of intervention are still very far from perfect, the evidence is encouraging. For instance, Patterson, after observing the characteristics of parents who produced particularly aggressive children, has developed successful "parent training programmes", based on behavioural methods. Many other apparently different types of therapy also seem to work, so it is not clear yet what is specifically effective. It may be characteristics of the therapist, as much as the theoretical model they are following.

I should like to draw attention to a potentially promising concept developed in the UK. "Expressed Emotion" or "EE" is a rating derived from interviews with relatives of psychiatric patients, and has components of criticism, hostility and over-involvement. A large number of studies have shown that "High EE" is associated with poor outcome for people suffering from schizophrenia, but that relatives can be educated to be less critical and this reduces the patient's disturbance. Thus one of the psychiatric illnesses most likely to have a genetic or other organic cause, has a course which can be altered by family intervention.

From a clinical point of view, high levels of hostility and criticism, sometimes combined with over-intrusiveness, are immediately evident in some families with "problem children", as shown in the case histories. Research evidence is also showing that reduction of parental "EE" may help children, and this is something for parents to consider.

ARE "DISTURBED" CHILDREN MENTALLY ILL?

The "medical model" encourages doctors, like myself, to give disturbed children a "diagnosis" or at least assign their problem to some sort of category, such as "Emotional Disorder" or "Conduct Disorder". Classification systems do have their uses, but should not be taken to imply that everything is known about the causes or outcomes for particular sets of "symptoms" in particular children. It is remarkable how often, in fact, teachers' and parents' views may differ, or a child responds differently to a different school or teacher. An advantage of "labelling" is that sometimes it is the only way for a child to get access to the help she or he needs; a disadvantage is that it sounds as if the child has a permanent disability, when the difficulties may largely depend on the context, and be reasonably responsive to alteration.

Realising that children – and even parents – may change for the better despite all odds, may help disappointed parents move forward from a position of fixed gloom and blame, to seeing what they can do to improve the situation.

3

AGES AND STAGES

Different ages may present particular challenges to different parents. This chapter looks at four stages at which characteristic reasons for disappointment arise.

1. THE BABY

"A baby at birth is usually disappointing-looking to a parent who hasn't seen one before."
  Benjamin Spock

The first sight and holding of the new-born baby by the mother is a traditional moment of excitement and pride, often touched with a tinge of anxiety as well as wonder. Is she all right in all respects? Who does he look like? Sometimes there is an obvious reason for disappointment, for instance an evident abnormality, handicap or illness. There may or may not have been some preparation for this knowledge. In these circumstance parents have to face a major degree of disappointment from the start, but there is considerable professional understanding of this, and there

3

22

are many specialist organisations which can both support parents of handicapped children psychologically and offer information and access to specialised resources or facilities. It is well understood that parents of handicapped children have suffered a loss in terms of the perfect baby that was not born, and that feelings of grief and anger are natural. Parents often find it helpful to air and share their experiences with other parents in a similar situation, and and to take as positive action as possible. With a "label" such as Down's Syndrome, for instance, parents can learn what to expect. They find out how they can help their child to achieve its full developmental capacity and discover that children with the syndrome can survive well and be happy and loved members of their families.

Difficulties in babyhood, however, can be less obviously severe, or unclear, or lead a fluctuating course. Such uncertainties can be just as, if not more, difficult to adapt to.

When I used to visit a "special care" baby ward, for premature and other ill new-borns, I realised that the strains for the parents were often considerable. If the baby has been born prematurely it looks unattractive – thin and monkey-like instead of nicely rounded. Then the fairly unresponsive and sick little thing is likely to be in an incubator, and it is hard for a parent not to feel helpless. Sometimes it is "touch and go" for quite a while before it is even clear whether the baby will survive, and if so, whether with handicaps or not.

In my experience some parents step back a bit psychologically in such a situation, not knowing how much to let themselves get attached, in case they lose the baby. Meanwhile, staying at the hospital is stressful as it means having to neglect other family responsibilities, but you don't know if you're doing any good either. On the other hand it is stressful at home, when a telephone call from the hospital may bring alarming news. All this stress is increased, of course, when there are twins, as is not uncommon amongst premature births.

Shane was one of two premature twin boys. They had both been very small and ill at birth and had had to spend many weeks in the special care baby unit. Shane had an abnormality of his abdominal tract diagnosed even before birth and had to have an operation soon afterwards from which he took time to recover. He then gained weight slowly, was irritable and also had fits. The mother could not help comparing him unfavourably with his twin brother Samuel.

At the age of 16 months, but looking younger, they were both seen at the child guidance unit.

His mother saw Shane as more miserable and stubborn than his brother. He could not yet walk or talk, was slower than her other two children, and was always whining and wanting to be catered to.

Many aspects of her life had failed to turn out as she had wished. She had hoped to marry the children's father, but he now visited much less. She used to receive help with her older boy from her mother and sister, but they were now less helpful. The older boy, who used to be quiet and obedient, had now become "babyish". And yet the mother was not depressed, and was obviously competent with the older boy and the other twin. Sadly Shane, the less able twin, seemed to be the focus of her anger at life's disappointments.

The idea of bonding and attachment was perhaps overplayed at one time – as if it was a sort of "super-glue" event between mother and child that could be brought on or prevented quite simply. It is clear that the circumstances of the premature baby's care may make a steady, close emotional relationship between mother and child more difficult to achieve.

In the case of Shane his mother had a variety of other external pressures also, and she found it hard to respond supportively to this far-from-perfect child. This was exacerbated by the fact that he was always being compared unfavourably to his twin.

Sometimes a birth can produce an entirely healthy-looking baby, and yet as time passes, things do not seem quite right, but there does not seem to be anything obviously wrong. Parents do not wish to be criticised as "over-anxious" and may be unsure of what standards to expect, especially if they are dealing with their first child.

Nicholas had been a much-longed-for baby, who was first brought to see a child psychiatrist at the age of 18 months, but had been seeing many other doctors long before that. He had been born when his mother was 42, after many years of trying, and was the only child. He was born two weeks overdue and the birth had to be induced. However, he seemed completely normal and healthy and at first both parents were happy with their bonny baby boy.

But as the first months passed, Nicholas did not progress well. His head control was poor and he was not sitting by eight months. He did not seem to reach out as other babies do, and he was very difficult to feed, refusing solids altogether. By 15 months, although he could remain sitting he could not get himself to the sitting position, and he could only creep on his stomach rather than crawl on all fours. He was only saying a few small words, such as "dada", "mama", and "don't", but testing showed that his hearing was quite normal. He was a good-natured child usually, who liked to be entertained and responded to his own name, but he was still very difficult about eating anything solid.

Nicholas was having a variety of tests and investigations, but so far there had been no abnormalities found to explain the developmental delay.

When I met the parents they were in a state of some confusion. On the one hand they could see for themselves that their child was not developing nearly as fast as other children, but he looked an attractive and normal child. They were also getting fed up with being told optimistic things such as that he would soon catch up. In search of a label they were wondering if Nicholas could be considered autistic.

It is now acknowledged how difficult doctors find it to "break bad news". And even if they have actually given a diagnosis (the name of the disorder or disease) or prognosis (the probable outcome), the parents may not have heard or understood them.

It often takes parents a long time to accept and come to terms with a handicap. In some ways this response can be to a developing baby's advantage, as everybody seeks to be optimistic and do all they can to help. However, sometimes parents feel that their concerns are not being appropriately recognised. It can be very stressful to have hopes continually raised through reassurance, only to have them dashed.

Nicholas's parents had begun to search for a more systematic explanation such as "autism" as something they had at least heard of, and perhaps could begin to deal with. Although there are a variety of definitions of "autism", it is usually confined to individuals whose handicap is in the sphere of language and social communication. Nicholas had severe developmental delay all round, not just with speech, and had mental handicap or "severe learning difficulty" as it is now termed. He is now walking, and talking more, but is likely to remain "slow" and in need of much special support, which he is now receiving at school.

2. THE TODDLER

"You sowed a baby and you reaped a bomb."
  D.W. Winnicott

Babies usually have an intrinsic "Aah" factor, due to their cuddly softness, roundness, their dependence and soothability.

However, the next stage of development entails not only the exciting mastering of the skills of walking and talking but the potential for the communication of defiance and anxiety by tantrums and destruction.

Parents may have "read up" this stage, but nonetheless be astonished at the powerful emotions stirred up by the little beast in front of them. They were never going to smack their children, only be pleasant and use reasoning ... but suddenly they have smacked them, and they feel angry with themselves, their partner and the child. This was not the way things were supposed to turn out ...

Joe, three, was brought to the hospital child psychiatry clinic by his parents. As they were both teachers they found it somewhat embarrassing that they were unable to cope with their own child. They described Joe as very obstinate and difficult. For example, if he did not get his own way he would have a temper tantrum. He seemed to have become much more demanding in the last 18 months or so, but had always been difficult to manage and fractious. He commonly woke up three or four times a night, and sometimes more often. It was very hard anyway to get him to settle down to sleep, as he became very clinging and did not want his parent to leave. He refused to sleep in his cot after his parents had once left him to cry there, and since then he had slept on a mattress on the floor. He was usually put to bed by his father who played with him or read a story and had to stay until Joe actually fell asleep. He still sometimes wanted, and was allowed, a bottle if he was upset or tired.

The parents found it very hard to manage Joe's behaviour and felt that it was their disagreement over his management which was making things worse. The father tended to be more calm in his approach, and the mother firmer, but she could over-react by smacking.

The parents had been married for ten years before the arrival of Joe, after considerable anxiety and ambivalence over whether or not they should have children. The mother, especially, had wanted to delay parenthood, because she wished to extend her professional career first.

The pregnancy was normal and uneventful. Labour was 12 hours long, culminating in a forceps delivery because of foetal distress. A poor neonatal experience followed for both mother and child as Joe was very inactive for the first few days. He then became very fractious, by which time the mother was anxious about breast-feeding and at odds with the hospital, which was trying to get her to use a bottle. At the hospital's insistence mother and baby stayed in

29

hospital for eight days. The parents were still rather angry about the way the hospital had handled things.

Once at home Joe began to feed well, and this continued for a month, but he then had episodes of vomiting which took some months to improve. As the mother found these early months very stressful, she felt she had to take a regular break from Joe and so returned to teaching two afternoons a week, leaving Joe with a child-minder.

Due to the poor initial state of the mother-son relationship, Joe formed a closer attachment to his father which still persisted. However, this relationship was not a straightforward one either. The father thought that Joe was over-aggressive, and worried that he was losing a battle with him. While he felt that Joe should not be as immature and demanding as he was, he found it difficult to take a firm line with him and tended always to give in to his wishes. The mother resented this, as she had to be the disciplinarian and this impaired her own efforts to have playful, pleasant times with Joe.

It was fairly clear that the mother's original ambivalence about the pregnancy and the poor neonatal experiences had contributed to a tenseness in the relationship with her son, probably compounded by temperamental factors.

It was the father, however, whose expectations of idyllic and easy parenthood had been most shattered. In some ways he had been left "holding the baby" and was finding it most trying – being kind did not seem to be working very well, and furthermore his wife was blaming and criticising him for the situation. Joe's behaviour was not, in fact, especially aggressive for his age, but his night-time behaviour was showing a certain amount of insecurity, probably exacerbated by his parents' anxiety and inconsistency over his management.

Joe's parents were offered, and responded well to, a few sessions of family therapy. This mainly aimed at giving some support, and advice if requested, to help this otherwise competent pair to find their own agreed methods of dealing with their small son.

Dionne was three when she was brought to the clinic with her younger brother by her parents. Her mother complained that she had temper tantrums in which she screamed continuously and wrecked the flat. If punished, she would continue to scream and then do something worse, such as throw the cat litter all over the house or spray water on newly-ironed clothes.

Dionne had not yet started at nursery school, and so her mother looked after her all day. Unfortunately, Dionne started screaming if left alone even for a few minutes. She was quite stubborn – refusing to eat what she did not want to, and refusing to go to bed when asked. She had her own room but she insisted on sleeping with her parents, although it did not seem that she was afraid. She was still wetting the bed at night.

The father was currently unemployed but still did not

31

have much to do with the care of the children. The mother seemed to prefer this as she felt her husband had no patience with them. She was now pregnant with her third child.

In the interview, Dionne did not say much, but she seemed to be a happy child, playing well with her younger brother and not showing any signs of jealousy.

On investigating Dionne's history we discovered that she had started to become difficult about sleeping and eating when at the age of three months the family moved from London to her grandparents' home in Essex. During this period her father was away from home from six am until nine pm. As Dionne grew older she had begun to run screaming to her grandparents if she did not get her own way. They gave in to her, and the mother felt undermined and lacking in authority.

The behaviour just got worse when the family had moved away from the grandparents back to London, nine months previously. Both parents were quite angry and upset that when Dionne was sent to her grandparents and had their entire attention, the grandparents said her behaviour was no problem.

These kinds of symptom – of temper tantrums, and being very demanding are part of the battle for control which is characteristic of two- and three-year-olds. And of course, this is a common period for a new baby to arrive and be a cause of jealousy.

This family seemed to have been rather flummoxed by Dionne's apparent lack of jealousy, and by her demands, many of which were given way to. They could not understand her terrible, even hurtful behaviour. The fact that she could behave well for the grandparents only made matters worse in terms of both parents feeling quite inadequate. Again, a few further family discussion sessions were offered with good results, as Dionne's mother and father began to reflect on how to handle her better, and also decided to send her to nursery school part-time.

In Joe's and Dionne's cases the children were developing normally, and presenting the challenges of adaptation appropriate to their age. Their personalities doubtless made this even more difficult. Both sets of parents had fallen out over the management and limit-setting for demanding behaviour, and seemed very uncertain of themselves as successful parents. In neither case were the grandparents viewed as able to help – in Joe's case because they were rather distant emotionally, and in Dionne's because their relative success made the parents feel dispirited.

Parents can easily feel uniquely incompetent about their own small children, and it is helpful to get together in groups with other parents, even if just in the park. You will then notice that other children misbehave too – which can be quite a relief – and that you can exchange ideas on topics such as smacking, or television, or just how ratty it can all make you feel.

3. SCHOOL EXPECTATIONS AND FAILINGS

"Two sisters by the goal are set, Cold Disappointment and Regret."
  Scott

For middle-class parents school is the major proving ground for their children. A lot of careful attention has been given to them in their earliest years, and now they have to face the real challenges of survival in a less familiar and less nurturing environment. While many children take readily to school, particularly if they have had some experience of nursery education, others find the strain of large groups of children very difficult to cope with, especially if the "lunch hour" is long with little supervision. Some children seem to get into trouble for what their parents had previously considered to be their strong points ...

Vincent's parents had been encouraged by his school to get him referred for "help", as he seemed to be rather an odd and isolated little boy, who never quite "caught on" to what was expected and preferred to follow his own way. He could be openly defiant of the teacher's authority and would not accept any criticism. He was obviously quite intelligent, and his reading and language were ahead of many of the other children. However, he did not get on with other children, and often there were little squabbles and fights between him and the other boys. He did respond well to one-to-one attention from an adult, but this is difficult to provide in a class of 25 children.

Vincent's parents were quite upset by the trouble their only child was getting into, and thought the school must be exaggerating and picking on him. When he had been at nursery school part-time, his teacher had thought he was very bright, and had taken special pains with him.

Vincent's father and mother were both working full-time, and his grandparents had looked after him a lot. It seemed that the considerable amount of positive adult attention that Vincent had been used to was suddenly withdrawn in school, and he was finding it hard to adjust.

This kind of difference of point of view between parents and school can arise easily, and be difficult to resolve without a bit of give-and-take on both sides. In this case, the doctor involved went along to the school and observed Vincent in the classroom, just to see exactly what was going on. He then met with the parents and the teachers so that they could all work out ways of approaching the problems constructively. As is often the case, a discussion with the parents and teachers together helped to make everyone aware of the situation and, even just that can bring about improvements.

Another bright little boy whose first terms at primary school went badly wrong was Aidan.

Aidan was also an only child, who had seemed to be reasonably happy at his nursery school. But when he started at school full-time, he began to get into trouble for refusing to do what he was told and getting into fights. He was not making the educational progress his mother expected of him, and started to wet the bed at night and even sometimes poo in his pants.

At first Aidan's mother thought there was something physically wrong with Aidan, as he had had a nasty bout of diarrhoea when the family had been on holiday. However, the problems just seemed to continue, and Aidan clammed up about school when his parents asked him about it.

After the family had attended the clinic a few times and began to relax about the whole situation, it emerged that Aidan had been quite seriously bullied and become very unhappy but had not told anyone about it. His mother went to the school to speak to the head and the teacher, and things did improve a little. Aidan, however, who by now was much more communicative, said he was still not happy at school, and his parents decided to transfer him soon after their planned move of house.

Aidan's parents decided for themselves to try to find out just why their son was not doing as well at school as they had hoped, and fortunately were able to resolve and improve things. It is a dilemma for parents whether always to back their children fully and assume that the school is at fault, or the reverse. Some parents oscillate between the two explanations! In the triangle that exists between the parents, the school and the child, parents often feel blamed by the school, and this can make things difficult to sort out. However, calm discussion between the adults concerned can nearly always improve matters, and helps the child to feel more secure again.

Moving on to the next stage – the agonies around the choice of secondary education are well known. The local state school has some possible social and definite short-term economic advantages, but can special allowance be made for reading difficulties? Is bullying controlled? What is the university entrance record like? On the other hand one's child can also fail to get in to the desirable private school, or opt out and fall into bad company while there, thus wasting money as well as time.

Rachel was referred at the age of 12 for refusal to attend school. She had first attended a slightly distant mixed comprehensive for half a term only, then a more local mixed comprehensive which she attended for one day only. Rachel was an attractive girl but she was rather dowdily dressed, more in the manner of a primary school than a secondary age child. She seemed precociously intelligent yet also anxious and confused, becoming more clearly unhappy as the interview progressed. She was quite clear what the trouble was. She was the only middle-class child in her year and was picked on by her peers for her clothes, her accent and her interests. Her parents had tried to intervene

37

*but this had only led to more victimisation. Finally Rachel
had stayed in bed and refused to go.*

*The parents were a rather gentle, idealistic couple. The
father was a musician and the mother worked as a
librarian. They spoke softly in an academic and reasonable
way. The family said they felt different from other local
residents, and that this could account for Rachel's lack of
friends. The parents felt they might be more at home in
Hampstead rather than South London.*

*However, the father's view was that Rachel needed
education for "the social experience". They had
specifically chosen the first secondary school because
Rachel had wanted a co-educational school and the parents
thought that it had "a liberal regime". The second school
was also co-educational, and they had taken pains to ensure
that it had a good music department, where Rachel could
continue her violin lessons and have the opportunity to
take part in an orchestra.*

Rachel's parents were hoping that she could progress in a
social environment they had simply not prepared her for,
being rather isolated in their own neighbourhood.

They were right in thinking that she had qualities which
would be appreciated by good secondary schools, and the
teachers in each school had done their best to encourage
and protect this rather awkward, bookish girl. Rachel was
probably trying to live up to her parents' expectations at
first, and found it difficult to reveal the extent of the bullying

that was going on. Her parents did not really seem to want to hear about her social problems. They felt their daughter's attitude to the other pupils was rather snobbish and that it was her own fault if she was unpopular.

After two interviews, in which at least a variety of family views had been aired, Rachel's parents decided to look into the possibility of other local schools with the help of the education welfare service. Fortunately, there was a nearby all-girls school which was able to make a place available for Rachel, and with some carefully arranged support she did settle in.

Michael's problems centred round his school homework. He was 12 and the only child. Both parents were working in demanding full-time professional jobs, the father as a doctor and the mother as a lawyer. As it was quite clear that Michael was an extremely able boy, they were beginning to think that his evident lack of organisation was perhaps some sort of disorder – like dyslexia.

However, the "problem" really only showed itself in relation to school. Typically Michael "forgot" to write down or do his homework, and "couldn't find" his sports equipment when it was time for school. The parents had unsuccessfully, both separately and together, tried to prompt, remind, nag and supervise him. On the other hand, "ignoring" the issues had also failed. This had led to considerable trouble at school, both directly for Michael – to which he seemed fairly oblivious – and for his parents, who were often being called in. Michael described a "split" amongst the staff: some of the teachers wanted to threaten him with expulsion, but others were more sympathetic.

No other difficulties were remarked on, except "lack of communication" within the family. Michael had several friends with whom he shared similar interests, such as listening to "heavy metal" rock music on the local pirate radio stations.

To his parents it already seemed quite possible that Michael would be expelled, or not do well enough in his GCSEs, would drop out, not go to university, and probably irreversibly ruin his prospects in life. They were worrying about this a great deal, while Michael didn't seem to care at all.

The family had no other major stresses, and the background was unremarkable, except perhaps that there were hardly any close relatives in the country, as both parents had been brought up abroad.

In the interview the mother and father sat closely on each side of Michael, with the father patting his hand from time to time. Almost the only topic was Michael's homework, but his parents seemed to be pulling back from expressing just how angry and upset it made them feel, apparently in an attempt to "shield" their son. It was evident that the situation was making the mother in particular feel desperate and in some way to blame, while the father felt helpless. Michael smiled a great deal, like a cute and naughty baby.

As we shall see in many other cases, their son unerringly "pressed the right button" for these parents in a way that ensured that he gained the greatest possible attention and became the focus of all concern. Yet these were not the type of parents to lay blame, and this was partly why they were thinking of a "medical" explanation, as a face-saving scenario all round, and one also with the possibility of "cure". Perhaps Michael felt that some of the time his parents spent professionally on other people's problems could be usefully diverted on to him.

Michael and his parents attended for further family discussions, and began to focus on the importance of allowing Michael to take increasing responsibility for his homework, as he already had some fairly clear goals of his own – in line with his parents'. There were a number of ups and downs over the next two years, but basically the parents began to find out how not to make the "homework" situation even worse by attempting to control it, and were able to focus on other more positive aspects of Michael's progress.

TEENAGERS

"The girls nowadays display a shocking freedom; but they were partly led into it by their mothers, who, in their turn, gave great anxiety to a still earlier generation."
Edmund Gosse

41

Even the word "teenagers" seems to bring with it implications of threat and menace, as if there were a uniform, alien sub-culture out there. And certainly those teen years from 13 to 19 can be some of the most testing for parents. What are parents hoping for as the outcome of this stage?

Of course, parental expectations vary. But usually they hope that their children of both sexes will have a good grounding for earning their future living, for instance that they will have started further education or training, or have a job.

Some parents who went through a vaguely hippy-ish or counter-culture stage in their own youth, may be keen to see evidence of something similar in their own children (not taken to extremes, of course). Most parents wish their nearly-adult offspring to be happy and taking a growing responsibility for themselves. They also want their relationship with them to be maintained in reasonable harmony.

WHAT ARE THE FEARS OF PARENTS OF TEENAGERS?

These are usually readily articulated. If there must be early sexual activity and sexual experimentation, please let it not be of the kind to result in AIDS or pregnancy. Please let James and Jane stick to their school work, not fail their exams, not leave home to live in a squat, not take to drugs, not become the victims or perpetrators of crime. And on a lesser scale – not refuse to wash, not disgrace the family, not retire to their room all the time nor stay out all night, and so forth.

So much of importance seems to hang in the balance in these years, that even though parents may know in theory that "all teenagers are difficult", in practice they could still be disappointed. It can also work the other way, so that the first signs of appropriate individuality, such as arguments over clothes, seem to escalate into a threat of future certain delinquency or permanent disruption of the parent-child relationship.

Claire was referred by her GP when she was 13, and was seen with her parents, Mr and Mrs Jones, and her older brother Paul, aged 15. Claire was being very defiant both at home and at school, causing particular problems to her mother.

Mrs Jones found that rules such as Claire telling her where she was going, coming in on time and so on were being ignored, and rows would occur on confrontation. On one occasion, Claire stayed at a friend's house for two nights without telling her parents, which naturally worried them a great deal.

Since the mother and daughter had a recent "heart-to-heart" things had improved a bit. There had been tears on both sides.

Claire was described as an outgoing person who readily made friends, although her mother disapproved of the way many of them were apparently allowed so much freedom by their parents. She attended an all-girls school which was quite strict – for instance there were rules about going only "oneway" down certain corridors which she often got into trouble for breaking. The school had, in fact, decided to change her class that term, because of the extent of her bad behaviour. On the other hand, her academic work was average, and Claire was aiming at A level in Art and Design.

Mrs Jones was in her 30s and was now working part-time arranging conferences. Two years before, she had been through a period of considerable stress when her mother, aged 70 and ill with diabetes, had to be admitted to a psychiatric unit for six months. As she was the only child and her father had died of cancer some years before, it seemed to her that she had to take a lot of the burden alone.

Claire's father worked as Managing Director for a small company, which meant that he often had to work long hours and travel abroad, but his relationship with the family was a positive one.

Paul was doing very well at school and was altogether a quieter and less troublesome type than his sister. In the interview session he was quiet and polite, and answered questions if asked. He denied ganging up on Claire, but did say he thought the rules were reasonable, and that she was often quite rude and aggressive to their mother.

Claire looked and sounded unhappy, but said very little. She confirmed her mother's guess that she felt Paul was getting all the positive attention. She had been very worried about her grandmother, and still did worry a bit about that. She denied other worries, and did not really account for her general attitude towards rules. Mrs Jones was critical of Claire, but also described her with some warmth, and seemed sad at having lost a previously good relationship. She was keen to stress improvement, as if perhaps there had been no need to come. She said she realised that Claire's friends' mothers might be less strict, but felt her own rules were very reasonable.

I felt that a tense relationship had developed between this teenage girl and her mother which was mainly being expressed in rows over rules at home and at school. Both seemed unhappy about the situation, and the family was otherwise functioning well. While the severe illness of the maternal grandmother was the clearest stress on the family, it seemed possible that the father had become more emotionally distant, partly because of work pressures. In response to this one could observe the older brother taking a somewhat inappropriately parent-like line with his sister, and so perhaps he had become more of his mother's support when she was under emotional strain.

Both parents were keen to discuss whether their own expectations of behaviour were reasonable, despite their daughter's claims, and when offered support, used it very readily. Claire, being a bright girl, could see that a family rule about telling people where you were, was protective,

45

and indicative of care – of a somewhat different order than not running down school corridors. In this case, the main issue was to restore parental confidence in their limit-setting abilities, which is always tricky to negotiate when one is at the same time hoping to encourage independence and self-responsibility from the young person. The parents found the support they needed in just a few sessions and also felt confident that the improved communication they had achieved with Claire over this crisis period would help them to resolve future difficulties.

Kathy was referred by her school head of year at the age of 15, and attended the child guidance unit with her mother and father. The problem was that, whereas she had previously been one of the top achievers in the school, she had begun to truant and her academic performance had deteriorated badly. At home she would not confide in her mother as she had done previously, say where she was going or what she was doing. Her mother suspected unsuitable involvements with boys but Kathy strongly denied this.

Her parents felt, on reflection, that the problem probably dated back two years previously, shortly after they had separated. Gradually Kathy had begun to skip lessons, and lose interest in her work. The parents had gone to the school together and Kathy had been put "on report". This did result in some improvement at first. Kathy was the oldest of three girls. As a baby she had been "very good" and had developed well. She had always been the quiet, shy, compliant and responsible one, leaving "naughtiness" to the younger two girls. In the interview Kathy said she felt very sorry for both her parents, and what they had gone through. Although she felt very sad that her parents had separated she accepted things as they were, and would not want her father back because of the rows. She seemed sad and spent most of the interview drawing and writing "I can't believe it's over."

This is a rather sad tale of a series of disappointments for the parents. First their own marriage broke up, and then their first and highly achieving daughter seemed also to fall apart. Although Kathy was not blaming her parents, they must have felt it was their fault in some way. Fortunately, all had come together to seek help, and Kathy did begin to feel more positive about school, and life in general once again.

The effects of divorce and parental separation on children are now more clearly understood. It can be "better" for children to be away from a situation of constant parental conflict, but divorce does not always bring this about, and anyway, children are often quite distressed and unhappy, although this may be masked, for instance by rebellion or misbehaviour.

Perhaps the extra significance of teenage problems is that the parents may be starting to feel that it's too late for them to alter things, as soon their young will be leaving home.

47

Some parents react by being disappointed and angry with their errant child; others are more inclined to blame themselves, and are upset at the loss of an image they may have previously had of themselves as being good, successful parents.

Like any other particularly "difficult" stage, however, there is nearly always a before and after of happier times. Teenagers can, and do, change radically once problems are identified and discussed. Their understanding is probably far greater than their parents give them credit for. And even when teenagers complain about and to their parents, they are actually secretly grateful for their concern, and welcome their support and guidance.

4

WRONG FROM THE START

"I beheld the wretch – the miserable monster whom I had created."
Mary Wollstonecraft Shelley

After the nine months of hopeful expectation from the mother-to-be, but before the arrival of the baby, come hours of labour. For some first-time mothers, this may be an unpleasant shock. Relaxing and breathing correctly, while helpful, do not always make pain bearable, and certainly do not avoid the difficulties which are sometimes part of the birth process. Mothers and fathers who had planned a "natural" birth, wanting to do the best for their baby, find they have to agree to other courses of action – and fast. Even if all then goes well, but especially if it doesn't, it may be hard not to feel disappointed and want to blame someone or something. There are plenty of possible candidates – the antenatal class, a particular doctor or nurse, the mother for being "weak", or the father for not being helpful enough.

Although at this stage the main "cause" – the baby – is not usually overtly blamed, if other factors are also present there may be a tendency later to associate the disappointment with him or her, as the case histories below show.

Elaine, who was 14 years old, was first seen in the child psychiatry department following a hospital admission for taking an overdose of paracetamol tablets. Her recent problems seemed to have started at the age of 11 when she was transferred from a state primary school to a more academic private girls-only school. Both her parents were graduates and wanted their children to have the best possible chance of obtaining a university education. At her new school, however, Elaine was unhappy and was usually at the bottom of the class. Her mother felt that Elaine was not performing as well as she could academically. She described Elaine as lazy and disorganised, unpredictable and inconsistent. She felt that she had to be constantly nagged, because "If she wants to do something she will do it very well." The mother's expectations of, and attitudes towards, the younger two girls were very different. She seemed much more able to allow them to behave as children.

On enquiring about Elaine's previous medical and personal history from her mother, we heard that the birth was traumatic. The mother had had a very difficult pregnancy in the course of which an ovarian cyst was detected. The baby was induced and delivered prematurely at 26 weeks. She had breathing problems – "respiratory distress syndrome" – which required incubator care for two weeks and so the mother and baby were separated. The mother then underwent surgery for the ovarian cyst. Subsequently the neonatal period was difficult and in the first year there were both sleeping and feeding difficulties. Elaine was an irritable child who cried constantly.

Although it might sound exaggerated to suggest that a difficult birth could "cause" a suicide attempt years later – and no doubt there were many other contributory factors – it was notable how very quickly the mother brought up her memories of this experience. It seemed that one of the major themes of the long-term negatively charged relationship was of a failure to live up to expectation, which was deeply hurtful to both.

While the mother cared deeply about her daughter, her concern came out mainly in the form of pained criticism. This meant that Elaine was unable to communicate her unhappiness verbally, and she resorted to taking an overdose instead.

This is not an uncommon way of coming to the attention of child mental health services, even for middle-class families, and an overdose, because it is such a fallible way of attempting suicide, often represents a cry for help rather than a wish to die. It can also feel like quite an aggressive act, and be extremely horrifying and shaming for parents. Sometimes families feel so disgraced that they even give a false name. However, most parents respond well to the crisis and use it as an opportunity to establish better communication and functioning within the family, to ensure that such a thing never happens again. Fortunately, Elaine's parents were willing to listen more directly to Elaine's needs and to start to help her feel happier within the family and at school.

Although the whole family had been invited, as is usual, Mrs King attended the clinic accompanied only by Brian, aged nine. Her distress about her son was immediately evident as she began to pour out her feelings in front of him. She could not and never had been able to love Brian and this "went back to the day he was born", she said. And now, Brian was behind with his reading, disruptive in classes and didn't want to study. He was overactive and always talking – even when asleep he talked and rocked all the time – which Mrs King found almost unbearable. He always wanted to be the centre of attention, and could never keep quiet and concentrate on anything by himself. He had to be nagged before he would do anything. He also fought constantly with his older brother Charles, whom Mrs King described fondly as "the favourite of the whole family". Nevertheless, Mrs King said, she did try to be fair in her treatment of both boys, but this just made Charles suffer as well if she tried not to show him more affection than Brian. She described herself as being able to look after Brian's physical needs, for instance if he was ill, but she felt she neglected him emotionally. At times she wondered if he wouldn't be better off being looked after by his father.

The family had financial worries and to Mrs King it seemed that Brian had tried and almost succeeded in breaking up her second marriage after only one year. Her father had died the previous year and she still missed him a lot, although they also had argued a great deal.

Mrs King had married her first husband young and against the advice of her parents. They had stayed together for 15 years despite continual arguments. This was reminiscent of her own childhood in which her parents also rowed a lot, and she remembered being very jealous of her younger sister who seemed to be the favourite.

The pregnancy and birth were described as an almost totally bad experience. Mrs King almost miscarried three times, the worst occasion being when she was five and a half months pregnant and was hurt in a car crash. She felt that her husband had been totally uncaring about this. Brian's birth was long and painful – 15¹/₂ hours labour, 36 stitches and 12 hours before she actually saw her baby, at which point she felt nothing for him. The weeks and months following the birth were unsettling. Brian had been re-admitted to hospital with jaundice and then she and Brian had had to go and live with her mother because of housing problems. Mrs King said she was in a terrible state during this time, and at one point recalled having just "snapped" and hit Brian. She found it hard to recall anything good about these early years.

Again, a crisis point in family life was connected with events surrounding the pregnancy and birth of the difficult child. Mrs King obviously felt guilty about her lack of positive emotion towards her younger son, and wished she could behave differently, yet her feelings, especially when there were several other stresses, were too strong.

To us, from the outside, it seems clear that Mrs King had been let down more by her husband and circumstances than by her baby, but perhaps little Brian's own difficult personality had been the last straw in preventing her attachment to him being a good one. By the end of the initial interview, Mrs King had begun to feel calmer and more confident at the clinic, and she agreed that her older son and her new partner should also attend further appointments. This, in itself, allowed for the intense negativity focused on Brian to be diluted, and the family were able to start to look at more positive ways forward.

The mothers in the two previous case histories were angry with their children and highly critical of them, though at the same time being desperately aware that a variety of factors had made their feelings towards the children tense from the start. Sometimes, as with the next case study, there is more obvious unhappiness and anxiety as well.

I saw Jill at the age of five because of her extreme shyness. She had difficulty in making friends of her own age and was very reluctant to speak in school at all. Her small private school had drawn this to the attention of her parents, as they were concerned that she was not coping. Her parents reported that Jill could also be very moody and difficult at home, although less so during the holidays. They were becoming extremely preoccupied with their daughter's lack of success, and compared her unfavourably with her younger brother.

Jill had been conceived after years of trying and even thoughts of adoption. The pregnancy was normal, but the birth was by Caesarean section for "failure to progress" in labour. Afterwards the baby was well, but the mother was quite ill with abdominal problems for one week. Once the pair were back at home, Jill was wakeful and irritable and needed lots of attention. Although her early milestones of development were normal, her speech was poor in its articulation and the necessary speech therapy sessions had been an irritation for the family.

Both parents were well-qualified professionals to whom achievement was important, and they felt that their daughter was showing early signs of both below-average intelligence and emotional disturbance. This could have been a realistic appraisal, but interestingly, when more detailed questions were asked, the parents themselves turned out to have had rather similar early histories. The father had been very quiet, shy and hated parties. The mother had been so shy that she didn't speak for her first year at school. This characteristic reserve was evident, indeed, even in the interview, but had not occurred to the *parents either as a possible explanation for their daughter's behaviour or as a sign that things might not turn out so badly after all in the end.*

These parents had tried hard for this birth. It had been a difficult experience, and now the child they had so much looked forward to seemed to be letting them down. Echoes of the midwife's announcement of "failure to progress" seemed to be still on their minds.

As with the other cases in this chapter, the child who seemed to be the focus of extreme parental disappointment had not only started off badly but was continually being compared unfavourably with another child or children. One reason why parents might compare children is to reassure themselves that they are not bad parents. The fact that they have and can love a "good" child reassures them that it is not entirely their fault.

Even so, these parents, with their marked "Negative Expressed Emotion" as described earlier, were very far from rejecting or neglecting their children. On the contrary they were very conscious of the difficulty and, albeit at a point of extreme stress, had decided to seek help.

Jill's parents in fact responded very well with just a few interviews. They began to see how their daughter in many ways resembled each of her parents, and that it was by no means a foregone conclusion that she was a complete failure. As they relaxed a little, so did Jill, who started to do better at school and even to make a few friends.

5

JUST LIKE ... THE BLACK SHEEP

"There is a black sheep in every family."
  Proverb

"Let him go for a scapegoat into the wilderness."
  Leviticus

In the past, a black sheep, which tended to be rare in a mainly white flock, was regarded as less desirable because its wool would not take a dye well. Now we use the phrase to describe a sort of uncharacteristic genetic freak, from whom the rest of the family can dissociate itself.

  A scapegoat, on the other hand, was an animal chosen by lot for the ritual purpose of bearing the sins of the tribe. It was driven out into the desert and so, by its punishment, alleviated the guilt of the people. In family terms, one might ask, is the "black sheep" a "scapegoat"? That is to say, is the fact that one member of the family is considered "bad" an advantage to other members, who are regarded as "better" by comparison?

  Sometimes, consciously or unconsciously, the child who reminds a parent strongly of some other family member who harmed or disappointed them, remains a negative focus. This is particularly common for boys whose fathers have somehow been unsatisfactory for their mothers, who often fear that the boy is turning out the same, and yet repeat the pattern of behaviour that may induce just this.

Chris, aged nine, attended the clinic with his mother and younger brother. He was not having major difficulties in school ("naughty but not terrible") but at home he was often openly angry with his mother, telling her he hated her. Mrs McDonald, Chris's mother, described him as arrogant and prone to telling lies. He often "wound up" and bullied his brothers. He had run away and threatened to kill himself. His mother thought the main cause of his unhappiness was his father, who took little interest in him.

Chris had been referred when younger with very similar problems. He had, in fact, been very difficult from the age of three. However, at that time, his mother had not kept up with treatment because she was overwhelmed with other outside pressures.

Mrs McDonald now had a second son, by another partner, Tom. She had broken up with him because he was possessive and jealous; but he did at least keep in touch with his child a little.

However, in Mrs McDonald's view, Chris's father (also called Chris) tried to avoid paying any maintenance although he had a good job. She thought he only made contact to blame and harass her. He was quite a bit older than Mrs McDonald, and the relationship had been a very strong one at first, but had later become increasingly violent. It made her angry that the younger Chris seemed to idolise his father and kept trying to ring him up. The older Chris was now living with a girlfriend, and had another son who was five years old.

Chris was an articulate child and told me happily what he liked and disliked at school. However, on home issues he became very reticent. He said "no-one listens to me or pays any attention to me" ; that was why he had hidden on Sunday and left a note saying "Sorry Mum, but I've gone for ever," with a picture of a tombstone. He acknowledged being sad and upset, and volunteered "angry" also. He drew a wrestler, and said that is what he'd like an imaginary dad to be like. When he grew up he'd like to be a football player. Chris and his brother agreed that it was sad that their dads had split up with their mum, and all were well engaged with the discussion.

Evidently Chris was a very unhappy boy, with symptoms of severe emotional disturbance and long-standing disturbed relationships with both parents. As sometimes happens with separated parents, the one who actually has most of the care of the children seems to come in for most of the blame. Chris did love and admire his father, and wanted to be like him, but his mother found this an unfair rejection of herself. At the same time she was still very angry with the older Chris, and to be reminded of him by his son was difficult for her to cope with. As with other cases, she had had unhappy experiences in her own childhood and hoped to do better as a mother herself.

In this case, we decided to focus on the mother rather than Chris, and a social worker started to see Mrs McDonald regularly to help her start to sort out her own feelings and ensure that Chris would also, as far as possible, have a continued relationship with his own father without his causing parental conflict.

Philip had been referred to the Child Guidance Unit by the Education Welfare Officer because of truancy. He attended with his mother and his younger sister Susie. Philip had been truanting from school for about one year, nearly always bunking off with friends. He lied to his mother about it when challenged and this had caused considerable tension at home. At school his reading was poor, and he had been recently suspended for having stolen a table-tennis bat.

He could be helpful but did not confide in his mother, with whom he seemed to have a tense but close relationship. He enjoyed sport, and going out to discos. He felt bullied sometimes at school though he did have friends and indeed a girlfriend. He often came in late, and had been picked up by the police once or twice. He admitted that a few of the boys he mixed with sniffed glue sometimes. His parents had married when quite young and had fairly rapidly had four children, of whom Philip was the second. The third had died from spina bifida at the age of 11 months. The marriage broke up when Philip was 11, after his mother discovered that her husband had been having an affair with her best friend. The climax came when the father had refused to go to see Philip when he was very ill with appendicitis. There was a violent row, his father left, and had only visited five times since. Mrs Abbott still suffered from pain from a slipped disc as a result of this assault.

Mrs Abbott was co-operative and articulate, but angry and convinced she was in the right. She admitted that she was stubborn and wanted the last word. She denied herself things for the sake of the children, and was both father and mother to them. She launched many verbal attacks on Philip and described him as being very like her ex-husband. She viewed his non-attendance at school as an attack on herself. Philip was quite a mature-looking 14-year-old who was reasonably assertive, but could not match his mother's verbal prowess. He didn't want to go to any of the local schools because of possible "trouble", but quite liked the idea of a small unit as described by the Education Welfare Officer.

Mrs Abbott was still feeling very angry and let down at the behaviour of her ex-husband. It is interesting that though Philip was now the focus of her anger, the final marital row had been about his care. Philip's current behaviour in a smaller way resembled that of her husband – he didn't tell her what he was doing or thinking and was getting into trouble. With the benefit of being outside the family, it was easy to see that Mrs Abbott was over-reacting somewhat, and probably making things worse by so doing. Just as she thought everything was bad about her ex-husband, so she now thought that this son was just like him. In reality he was anxious, and was very willing to try to improve his relationship with his mother.

The Abbots were all willing to come for further family discussions. It seemed that the safe setting of the clinic made it easier for them to begin to communicate with each other again without anyone having to storm out. As the immediate tension decreased, Mrs Abbott was encouraged to notice and talk about the things she did admire about her son. She also tried to "hold back" her extreme criticism of him, as she realised that it was not his fault if he triggered off painful recollections of her ex-husband.

Of course it is not always men who are the family black sheep. If it is a woman, there may be a girl who is apparently growing up to resemble her. The next case is obviously unusual in its details, but I have included it as a clear illustration of this process.

Tara, aged 14, had been referred by her GP to paediatric out-patients because of "tiredness". No serious physical reasons for this were found, and the symptoms had now considerably improved. However, the paediatrician noticed that Tara's grandmother, Mrs Phillips, who looked after her, was being extremely restrictive towards her grand-

daughter, who was beginning to resent this.

Tara attended a nearby mixed comprehensive, where she got on reasonably well. She wanted to be a mechanic (which was disapproved of by her grandmother), something to do with computers, or a secretary. The grandmother told Tara that if she wanted to go out with friends in the evenings she would have to live with someone else. Mrs Phillips made this rule because she was very religious and had high standards, and also because she feared very much that Tara was beginning to behave like her mother. She was determined to try to prevent this outcome.

Initially, Tara was looked after by her mother, but when she was about four years old her grandmother took over completely. Tara knew her father slightly but he did not contribute to maintenance or make contact, nor did his family.

Tara's grandmother, Mrs Phillips, was now in her sixties. She was an immigrant to the country, and was currently working in an old people's home. She had high blood pressure, and was a widow.

Tara's mother was the older daughter of two. Mrs Phillips said that she had tried to bring her daughter up to respect people, but she had "taken to drink". About two years previously, in some kind of alcoholic fracas, she had assaulted her boyfriend and was currently in prison. Her younger sister, by contrast, had no problems, and was working as a secretary.

Tara was a rather large girl, a little shy, but pleasant in manner when encouraged. She seemed uncertain of the details of what had happened with her mother, and said she was "confused". Her grandmother did nearly all the talking, and was in tears when she spoke of her feelings about her daughter. Even with repeated prompting Mrs Phillips was not able to say anything nice about her grand-daughter, only more about how much she had given to Tara.

Mrs Phillips was clearly trying desperately hard to prevent Tara from turning out like her mother, mainly by keeping her away from nearly all social possibilities, by criticism, and by insisting on church attendance. There was a danger of this becoming counter-productive, and the shame and distress surrounding the assault and imprisonment had also impaired family communications. Fortunately, Tara and her grandmother had already responded to help from the paediatrician, and were able to make further progress with therapy. They were seen together and encouraged to communicate more positively. Tara's grandmother was encouraged to allow her grand-daughter more age-appropriate freedom, so that gradually Tara would take more responsibility for herself. When Tara began to speak up for herself it was clear that she was not an antisocial or rebellious girl and wanted to achieve an adult life in line with the grandmother's values.

In these three cases the mother (or grandmother) has felt severely let down by someone they thought should have behaved better not only towards themselves, but also to the child who is now the object of emotional focus. The child then resembles the offender in the eyes of the carer, and arouses very strong emotions of love and hate. The child also seems to elicit a level of criticism which is distressing for both parent and child. All this may lead to a repetition of the past, which is exactly what they are trying to avoid. The situation closely resembles those which are formally rated as high "Expressed Emotion" mentioned in the research studies earlier.

Often, these families come to the clinic in a state of such high tension that the first and most useful thing we can do is not to be judgemental, but to listen while everyone has their say. Helping the parent in the grip of this powerful emotion can take quite a while. We hope that they will begin to realise intellectually and emotionally that their reactions may be disproportionately negative. Then, as tension decreases, we encourage the parents to notice any signs of an improved relationship. This provides an opportunity for positive change which is usually received gratefully by the child.

6

DON'T BE LIKE ME

"Do as I say, not as I do."
  Proverb

Sometimes it isn't somebody else that you hope your child won't turn out like – but yourself. You know about your own faults, fears, weaknesses, past mistakes and traumas, and on the whole you try to forget about them or deal with them quietly if necessary. If possible, you want to prevent your child having to cope with a similar situation, and if it crops up, you may try to behave differently, perhaps more sympathetically than the way you were dealt with as a child. However, at first, it may not always be easy to work out exactly what is going on ...

Fenella was six years old and was said to have "claustrophobia". This was manifested by her complaining of headaches and tummy aches, mainly as excuses not to go to school. She used to enjoy school when it was held in the church hall, but when it moved to a smaller classroom her enjoyment ceased. Her mother, Mrs Maitland, thought that there were too many children in the class for her daughter, and that the headteacher's old-fashioned way of running the school did not help. Fenella was born by forceps delivery; she was jaundiced and had dislocated hips. She was in hospital for three months with hip splints. Otherwise she was a "smashing" child. She had attended nursery school and had been quite happy there.

Her parents were both teachers, and had an older boy of ten years old. The family seemed to be close-knit, without other major worries except for Fenella's failure to settle at school.

It did not take long for Mrs Maitland to tell me that she considered herself to have claustrophobia, following an incident when, as a child, she was punished by her mother by being locked in a dark room. She still had attacks of claustrophobic panic but generally coped by avoiding busy and crowded places. She felt very anxious for Fenella because she perceived her as going through a similar experience. The father, on the other hand, had no such anxieties, had been to a big school himself and even liked shopping in busy streets. He was concerned about his daughter, but not to the extent that the mother was.

"Going to school" anxieties are, of course, very common. Children do seem to be more prone to this if there has been the kind of parental over-protection that may follow from an illness in infancy, as was the case here. What is important is what happens next.

Many families take steps to ensure that their small son

or daughter carries on going to school, but has some of their particular stresses removed. For instance, a teacher may be able to identify and stop bullying, or perhaps the child can come home to lunch for a while. It is most helpful if the parents and school can work together on the problem.

In this case something stopped the parents from taking "common-sense" steps. The clue lay in the inappropriate use of the word "claustrophobia". Mrs Maitland was the real owner of the "claustrophobia", but was identifying closely with her daughter's apparent suffering. Because she connected her own symptoms with her mother's punishing behaviour, she wanted to sympathise with Fenella, and was finding it difficult to be firm. She felt the school was to blame, and maybe thought the headteacher was another "punishing mother" she couldn't cope with.

We were able to help the parents see that it would be helpful, in the end, for their small daughter to learn to cope with the usual demands of school. They should also try to ensure that, wherever possible, serious stresses are avoided. We recommended that as a first positive step both parents should approach the school and work together on a constructive plan for Fenella. This in itself would be likely to relieve Fenella's anxieties. We discouraged them from thinking of Fenella's anxieties as a "disease" (which claustrophobia sounds like), as that might have the effect of increasing her worries.

In the clinic, I have most often found this sad failure of a "don't be like me" situation when a mother has discovered that her daughter, like herself, has been sexually abused. This has happened despite all the efforts she felt she had made to ensure that such a thing would never occur.

Sarah, aged 12, and her mother Mrs Williams were seen because of the severe family upsets and strained relationships that had persisted following Mrs Williams's discovery that her daughter had been sexually abused by the man she had been living with. The man had been sent packing, and Mrs Williams had now moved into what she hoped was a much more constructive relationship. However, even though she and her daughter had tried various forms of therapy, the tension between them had continued at a high level for four years. While there was a variety of other current stresses which added to Mrs Williams's feeling she couldn't cope, her daughter's demanding behaviour seemed to her to be the main problem.

Sarah was the younger of two children. Mrs Williams recalled that she had had episodes of illness associated with the pregnancy and birth and that Sarah had been a very clingy baby. When Sarah was two years old Mrs Williams had a collapsed lung and had to be admitted to hospital. Both still remembered Sarah being "dragged off" her mother and crying. When Sarah started nursery school part-time, separation was difficult for months, and separation anxiety had continued for many years.

Sarah had been sexually abused by her "step-father" from the ages of six to ten, when she finally told her mother. There had not been enough evidence for a prosecution, which still made Mrs Williams very angry. Sarah had problems with settling at secondary school. She recently got into trouble at school for hitting a bully, but this seemed to have been effectively sorted out by her mother, who also got her extra reading help.

Mrs Williams was now in the process of opening a craft shop and was considering getting married again. She told me that she had been sexually abused by her own step-father at a similar age to her daughter, and had felt under-supported then by her mother, who had not believed her. Indeed she was still angry and upset with her mother about this.

She had married Sarah's father young, and had originally seen him as gentle, good-looking, charming, persistent, and caring. Later on, however, he had become extremely jealous, moody and violent, and they had divorced when Sarah was three. He had subsequently died in a road accident, which obviously meant that he was no longer around as a potential support for the family.

At the first interview Mrs Williams was so distraught, and Sarah so reluctant an interviewee, that the session was entirely spent gaining their confidence. In later sessions both began to calm down and talk a little more clearly about what was distressing to each of them. Sarah was adamant that she was not going to be seen on her own or say anything about the abuse.

We were then able to agree some goals, focusing more on the present than the past, as they wished. These were:
*   i) for both to be less unhappy;*
*   ii) for Sarah to have a little more freedom of action;*
*   iii) for her mother to become more effectively assertive*
*   to get "space" for herself.*

It took a few sessions over the course of several months for the above goals to be achieved, in particular for the mother and daughter to let each other out of their sight more. This helped to make their relationship much more relaxed.

Not surprisingly, however, the past still very much loomed, in particular for Mrs Williams. She felt that although she always took everything on herself and worked herself to exhaustion for her family, she never seemed to sense much gratitude or help. She could hardly bear to stop and think how her own beloved daughter had been sexually abused just the way she had been. Perhaps it was this over-"busyness" which had prevented her noticing what was happening in the first place. She needed to reflect on what had happened not just to her daughter but to herself.

Eventually things improved so much between mother and daughter that Mrs Williams was able to accept some therapy for herself – it has to be said, much to her daughter's relief. Meanwhile Sarah had started to see a counsellor by herself at school, and this was going well.

It seems that only now is the secret of child sexual abuse within the family beginning to be discussed. One can only speculate as to whether, had people talked about it before, they might have been able to help prevent the same thing happening to the next generation of children.

NOT UP TO SCRATCH

"Gods! How the son degenerates from the sire!"
  Homer

"Greatness of name, in the father, ofttimes helps not forth but overwhelms the son; they stand too close. The shadow kills the growth."
  Ben Jonson

We can see from Homer how long-standing the idea is that a son can fail to live up to his father's great name and thus be a cause of disappointment. This may be so not only for his parents, but perhaps for the wider population as well in the case of a very famous and important father – particularly when some rights of succession are involved as with royalty, a great estate, or a major business. Ben Jonson is pointing out that it may be the very greatness of the parent that disables the son in some way.

  There are many reasons why a child is not, and can never be, exactly the same as its parents.

  For many human physical and psychological traits, the children will tend to the average between the parents. The consequence of this is of course that if, say, the father is very tall and dark, and the mother short and blonde, then the children by being of middling height and colouring may "fail" to be as striking as either of their parents.

However, each individual child is not an "average". The interaction of genes from the father and mother, means that a child is often genetically more "something" than either parent, and this may not necessarily be viewed by them as desirable. From the point of view of human adaptation and evolution, Nature seems to like to try out a variety of possibilities. Consider, for instance, a family of musicians: they are likely to have musical children. But if only one child is born, and he turns out to be tone deaf, the parental disappointment might be great, even if he later becomes a highly successful businessman.

What about two parents of equally high intelligence? Their children will not all have the same level of intelligence – the average of their parents. Generally high intelligence is likely, but any one child might have a lower intellect. Not all traits are completely dictated by genetic influence anyway. Although highly intelligent parents will tend to have more intelligent children, the "heritability" of intelligence is only 0.7; so there is not a perfect correlation.

There is also a range of environmental reasons why a child is not able to achieve in the same way as its parent. For instance, it has been found that first-borns are particularly high achievers, who attempt to live up to their parents' hopes and expectations, as they have had to give up the position of the indulged baby and only child. The reverse holds true to some degree for youngest children, who are said to have the worst prognosis in child psychiatry – obviously not because of any genetic fault but because their parents are more likely to protect them and spoil them beyond the age when this is appropriate.

It has also been shown recently that highly intelligent parents are more likely to have neurotic and anxious children, especially, although not only, if they are of lower intelligence. This is true not only of the middle classes, who might pressurise their children to get into the private school of their choice, but is a phenomenon across the social classes. Being "anxious" may of course impede achievement later on and may result in such a child doing less well than their parents.

Not even geneticists will be immune from hoping that their children will do at least as well as, if not better than, themselves. They too are liable to be disappointed when fate rules otherwise.

Janine, aged 10, attended the clinic because of a "mystery limp" which had been assessed by several doctors who said it was of psychological rather than physical origin. She had "turned over" her foot two months previously when running in the street but this minor injury was not thought sufficient to account for her current symptoms. Janine's mother was not certain what to make of the situation, whether to be sympathetic or cross with her daughter, whether to believe the doctors or not. Janine seemed to her to be well-adjusted in other ways, doing quite well at school, having friends and appearing to be cheerful. Nothing special had happened recently to disturb the family equilibrium.

The parents' marriage had split up three years previously and the mother now had a new relationship which was going well. The two girls saw their own father every fortnight, and this was described as being an amicable arrangement. They were said to like the new boyfriend.

As the family discussion proceeded it emerged that her mother's irritation with Janine was not new, and that the way in which she fell short of her mother's expectations was in her appearance. The mother was slim, attractive and blonde. She obviously spent a lot of time on her own appearance in terms of clothes and make-up, and worked as a beautician. There was something of "all girls together" about the three females in the family rather than of a mother with her two daughters. The younger girl, Sophie, was very like her mother – blonde, slim and attractive. Janine was not that different, but was slightly plumper and rather more quiet in personality. However, to her mother she was too fat and not lively like her sister. Her mother was highly critical of her.

Physical symptoms with no apparent physical basis may often start with a "real" injury or illness, albeit minor. However, the natural recovery and rehabilitation process in such cases does not progress in the normal way. Janine's limp may have got her more than her usual share of her mother's love and attention, which is why it continued. It was sad that her other different and more constructive qualities were not being noticed as much.

Fortunately, once the family were convinced that there was nothing seriously wrong with Janine's foot, the symptoms began to improve. The two lengthy family interviews probably also helped by encouraging the family to discuss their relationships with each other.

Mrs Carter had telephoned for a family appointment because of difficulties with her eldest son, Mark, aged 16.

Even observing the family before they spoke gave us an indication of the situation. The parents sat together with the younger brother, Simon, between them. Simon was neatly turned out in a conventional manner. He seemed very quiet and reserved. The little sister Meg sat close to her mother. Matthew sat as far away as possible from his parents. He was challengingly dressed with a bright red bandanna, dark glasses and a shiny black leather jacket with the words "acid rock" written on it. He also had a solid white circle painted on the toe of his right boot.

Mrs Carter did most of the talking. She started by saying that although Mark had an IQ of 140 he had given up on work at his school; he had been keen once but now seemed apathetic and depressed. She read out extracts from Mark's school reports, which she had brought along. The latest

77

one (after the GCSE exams) said that if his present attitude continued he "might as well not come back". Mark was now doing History, French and Art for A levels, but was "on probation" for the term.

At home, Mark came in on time and was not particularly disobedient "for a teenager". He smoked, but at his father's insistence went into the garden to do so. He occasionally went to the pub for a drink, and that was OK by both parents. He brought a girl home one night expecting she could stay but this was shocking and unacceptable to both parents. Once he had asked if he could come home late, but although his father agreed, this was overruled by his mother.

Mark sat quite coolly throughout the interview, one leg up on the other knee. He agreed he did the minimum at school, but didn't want to leave because all his friends were there. When asked who he turned to most often when he needed help and advice, he had no hesitation in turning to his mother and saying it was her. Beneath the cool he seemed angry, especially with his father, even though it appeared that it was his mother who was taking the firmer line with him.

Mrs Carter was warm, emotional and dominating in the interview, seeming to take on the entire problem herself and also wanting to talk about her own life, particularly that she had not been allowed to do A levels. Her own father had been a lawyer, and had died when she was 12. Mark's father was a successful doctor, and although *concerned at his son's relative failure, seemed to want to distance himself from the problem.*

After two family discussions, which they had seemed to find helpful, the family decided to manage on their own. A few months later we heard that Matthew had given up all his studies, and announced he was going into the music business – and was trying to get a job as a sales assistant in a record shop as a start. "After the stage of intense disappointment," his mother wrote to us, "it was almost a relief when all our worst fears were realised." It looks as if Matthew is unlikely to follow in the family mode of successful doctor or lawyer that his mother, especially, wanted for him.

Mrs Carter was partly hoping that Matthew could fulfil some frustrated desires of her own. Yet this mother and son were also very close, as the son was ready to acknowledge, rather to his mother's surprise. He may yet do well, one feels, and it is to the parents' great credit that they stuck by a positive and negotiating type of relationship with their son even when he seemed to be pulling away completely from what they had hoped for him. Although their specific ambitions for him were not likely to be fulfilled, they probably had sufficient flexibility to be pleased if their son was successful in other ways.

Sometimes hopes can be disappointed in a more cruel and permanent way, as when a subtle but severe handicap like autism becomes manifest. In such cases a child may at first appear completely normal and even, at times, show flashes of real intelligence, which highly-achieving parents would be hoping to spot and encourage.

Mr and Mrs Carroll brought their daughter Maria, aged four, to see me at the suggestion of their GP and provided me with copies of the many assessments which Maria had already undergone. They were both professionals and had gone to some lengths to look into the nature of their daughter's difficulties, but were less than pleased with some of the diagnoses and the types of special educational help that were being offered.

The parents showed me their daughter – who was sitting quite quietly doing a puzzle. They were convinced that she was of at least normal intelligence, that her delayed speech was improving, and that hearing loss had still not been absolutely ruled out. They therefore resented suggestions that their daughter might be autistic and had come to me for a second (at least) opinion. The Carrolls had read and heard about autism, but strongly argued that it wasn't the correct diagnosis for their daughter. However, Maria had several of the characteristics of autism: impairment of language development, lack of normal social interaction, behavioural difficulties when faced with new situations. Even though these were to some extent improving, Maria was still considerably impaired when compared with a normal child of her age.

In a way, the difficulty of the situation was partially an educational one. Maria's educational needs had been formally assessed, and she was considered to be a girl with severe speech and communication problems, who in accordance with her parents' wishes, could benefit from placement at a language unit attached to a mainstream school. Unfortunately, access to such special needs provision was now less well co-ordinated than previously, and the first school suggested had now withdrawn its offer of a place. They had then been offered two types of provision mainly intended for autistic children, and were not happy about what they perceived as the negativity of this category.

Mr and Mrs Carroll were desperately hoping that their daughter was basically normal, but had some remediable condition. Of course, they were quite right to leave no avenues unexplored, but at the same time they could not yet begin to face the likely alternative. In fact, the education system seemed to have gone out of its way to provide extensive reports concentrating on strengths as well as weaknesses, and to make very specific recommendations based on these findings rather than a global "diagnosis". The most likely suitable compromise appeared to be a nearby "language unit" which I knew dealt well with children whose difficulties had a range of origins, so that Maria could get the best possible help while the final decisions about normal or special school could be delayed.

That Maria was very unlikely to become a highly achieving adult, and that autism was probably the correct diagnosis, would emerge more slowly, and it would be easier for the parents to accept this over time.

It often takes quite a time for parents to adjust to the idea of having a child with learning difficulties, especially if there is nothing outwardly wrong with the child. This corresponds to the stage of "denial" described in situations of severe emotional trauma such as bereavement. Parents may go through a stage of anger as they try, with varying success, to look for causes and possible cures.

Parents do need to discuss their ideas and feelings both with each other and outside the family. Once there is a firm diagnosis, whether of autism or of mental handicap of some other kind, many parents find that the most helpful thing is sharing their experiences with other similarly affected parents, and by joining with them to try to improve conditions for their children, or raise money for further research. All of these are helpful ways of acknowledging the painful reality of the situation, but they are also ways of moving on from helplessness into positive and constructive action.

8

UNGRATEFUL BEASTS

"How sharper than a serpent's tooth it is/To have a thankless child."
   Shakespeare, *King Lear*

"Thou hast never in thy life/Showed thy dear mother any courtesy."
   Shakespeare, *Coriolanus*

"Thy life did manifest thou lov'st me not/And thou will have me die assured of it."
   Shakespeare, *Henry IV Part 2*

Shakespeare's plays contain a number of disappointed parents, the most famous being King Lear. The focus is often on the offspring's ingratitude, as in the quotations above. The age and stage of the members of the audience are likely to affect which generation they sympathise with!

   There's not much point in debating whether children should feel gratitude to their parents. Of course, parents do a great deal for their children, usually without thought of anything in return. Children come to realise this when they are grown up and are parents themselves.

While children may not be consciously or overtly "grateful", I find that most children are much more concerned about their parents than the parents realise. Sometimes our most useful function is showing parents this. However, some parents are particularly prone to interpret their children's behaviour as personal ingratitude when all that an outsider might notice is thoughtlessness or naughtiness. Such a situation is often complex, and it is not easy to offer simple advice about a change of approach.

David, aged 15, had been referred by his school because of behaviour problems and lack of concentration. Although he was thought to be of "top band" potential, he had been put down a year in class because of his immature behaviour.

His mother had a catalogue of complaints about him: at home he was rude and disobedient, he combed his hair for up to one hour, stayed in the bath for two hours, and used too much soap and bath foam. He played his radio too loud and wouldn't turn it down when his mother asked him. He went to bed late and was sometimes late for school. He complained he didn't get enough pocket money and argued that he should be allowed to go to discos. She thought he was mixing with the "wrong crowd".

The mother was now single with two sons in their mid-teens. She had divorced their father because he hit the boys and since then she had brought them up on her own. She had not contemplated re-marriage because of the children. At 17, the older boy, Tony, was treated and behaved like "the man of the family". However, he also rowed with his mother and complained that home wasn't suitable for entertaining his friends. The mother complained loudly about the behaviour of her sons, being especially stung by their ingratitude at her enormous efforts bringing them up alone.

However, we learned that the mother had the reputation of going to the school to protest about David and then not following the advice given. We were therefore a little wary of falling into the same trap.

The interviewer's hypothesis was that, as the older boy Tony prepared to leave home, David had to become more babyish in order to give his mother a continued purpose in life, and perhaps to maintain the involvement of Tony. Whether or not this was the case, the interviewer (taking a somewhat paradoxical line) agreed with the mother's complaints about the children instead of suggesting that she was being rather unreasonable. Subsequently, the mother rang the clinic to say that the boys had been offended and she felt it would be best to leave it.

Clearly, many of David's "wrongdoings" were trivial or normal by usual standards, and would have been accepted as typical though irritating teenage behaviour by some parents. However, it did not seem that the mother was just temporarily stressed and therefore over-reacting Unfortunately, she seemed to have settled into a pattern of complaining disappointment about her children. The advice of others, whether of contradiction, suggestion or support, did nothing to alter this. Furthermore, complaining about her sons provided the major focus of her life.

Although it was not difficult to realise that this mother did not really intend to change anything about the situation, there is a lesson for other parents here. If there is something about your children that you spend a lot of time complaining about, what are you trying to achieve? You may be entering a neighbourly "Aren't they awful" contest with a friend, or you may be trying to get some sympathy as the mistreated victim. In other words, is there something you are getting out of this? If there is, it may be okay, and the children may accept you as a nag or fuss-pot. If not, then do something about it. Explain how you feel to your children and tell them what you are and are not prepared to put up with. A third party, such as a therapist, can be very helpful here, either with making plans or to mediate in the process of negotiation so that it doesn't develop into the customary row.

Andrew, aged six, was referred by the family doctor because of temper tantrums. Once again, there was a very long list of complaints, mainly about how he insisted on getting his own way and how his parents felt powerless to resist and unable to control him. For instance, if he did not get what he wanted immediately, he would have a temper tantrum, kick and scream. This could escalate into kicking his sister, breaking windows and damaging walls. He refused to go to bed when asked, insisted on sleeping in his parents' bed, and had to wear nappies or he would wet the bed.

Over the last year he had also started to steal from home and from shops. He often disappeared from the house without telling anyone where he was going. His mother had tried to discipline him, but had mostly given up. His parents said they had tried everything including smacking, leaving him alone in his room and not allowing him to watch videos.

What was especially galling to Andrew's parents was that they felt that they had given him, and were continuing to give him, a lot. For instance, Andrew had everything he wanted in material terms; he was often taken out and received £10 a week in pocket money.

What made matters worse was that Andrew was very attached to his paternal grandparents who lived nearby, and he ran to them whenever he was disciplined or punished at home. They were apparently always on his side and gave in to his every whim.

There were no obvious past or present stresses for the family. However, although Andrew had always been rather demanding and difficult, he had got very much worse since the birth of his sister two years earlier.

At school he was described as a "model pupil", "brilliant and co-operative". This just seemed to make his mis-behaviour with his parents even more personal and unreasonable.

In the interview, Andrew appeared quite confident,

playing with his sister cheerfully. He did not respond to questions from the interviewer except to say "Don't know." However, he did interrupt his parents' account of his behaviour by contradicting them rather cheekily.

Putting this down on paper makes the whole thing sound a little comical. How could a six-year-old be allowed to ruin his parents' lives in this way? ("All he needed was a good smack" I hear an older generation saying!)

Nevertheless, having got into this distressing situation, the parents had come for help and support, and were ready to take some different action. We encouraged the parents to discuss with us and with each other what rules they wanted to set for Andrew, and then how to make sure that they enforced them consistently. At the parents' suggestion, the grandparents came to the next family meeting, so that they could take part in the plan and not undermine the parents' authority. We recommended that the parents began by asserting their authority in an area where they both agreed improvement was necessary, and one which they could actually physically control, such as not putting a nappy on their son any more. They should work out how to respond if the result was a temper tantrum, but carry on anyway. As Andrew was present while these new ideas were being discussed, he was not particularly surprised or distressed, and his behaviour started to improve very quickly. He realised that his parents could be firm, and this made him more secure and happy rather than less so. We were able to leave the "gratitude" issue aside, as relationships became more constructive all round.

Returning to Shakespeare's characters for a moment – how did they fare? King Lear and his daughters, the loving and ungrateful alike, are all dead by the end of the play, which proceeded to its tragic end as Lear persisted in his embitterment. Coriolanus's mother seems to be trying to make her son feel guilty, so that he will follow her advice on his military activity; it was a successful move on her part, but ultimately unwise. King Henry IV's comment burst out when, as he lay dying, he saw his wastrel son trying on his crown. Fortunately, it turns out to be a misunderstanding; they are reconciled and the son becomes the brave Henry V. As in real life, most of the younger generation, despite their apparent "misbehaviour", do love their parents, and given the opportunity are quite ready to show it.

9

IN A STRANGE LAND

"How shall we sing the Lord's song in a strange land?"
  Psalms

*"Each blames the place he lives in: but the mind is most at
fault, which ne' er leaves self behind."*
  Horace

The modern world is characterised by movement – often
families in search of a better life in another country. The
men and women who move are active and able members
of society. Yet often the host culture is less welcoming than
had been expected and there are many difficulties of
adjustment, from financial, employment and housing to
differences of language, manners and attitudes. In Britain
and the United States this century, there has been a pattern
of immigration in which the first generation has often had
to work hard at jobs which were beneath their capabilities,
but the second and third generations have moved up both
socially and economically. This almost inevitably means
that as the children adapt to the new culture they know
less about their parents' own culture, and can even neglect

or dismiss it.

Sometimes, however, the parents adapt more successfully to the new culture than their children do ...

Tony, aged 12, was brought to the clinic by his mother and grandmother. His mother said she was worried about Tony because after he started secondary school he began to fall increasingly behind in his school work, refused to do his homework and generally seemed sullen and difficult. His mother was very worried about the type of children he was mixing with. Family stress was increasing as the mother began to nag Tony more and more, while he became increasingly resistant to her pleas.

Although Tony had been born in England, his parents were both from the Caribbean. His mother was now well established with a responsible job as an office manager, and was engaged to be married again. She had come to this country to join her own parents when she was 15, and had taken a while to settle in. Her relationship with Tony's father had broken down after four years, and she now very rarely saw or heard from him. She had therefore brought up Tony largely by herself, with some help, especially in the early years, from her own mother.

She had just begun to reap the rewards of all her study and hard work. But Tony was letting her down in a major way, and might even be jeopardising her new relationship. The strain he was causing was affecting her concentration on her job.

Her mother very much sided with her, and both felt that they had been let down by Tony's father who was not around to give his son the male attention and guidance he needed. They also thought they had been let down by the British school system. They thought that Tony had had some difficulties with reading which had been ignored and that now, at the secondary school stage, Tony was being criticised for his behaviour. At times they felt that Tony was being unfairly picked on because he was black. They also thought that the school was not strict enough and that the old-fashioned discipline and lesser degree of racism in the West Indies would have been better for him. They did not feel they knew the staff at the school well enough to have a constructive discussion with them, however, and felt they were in an impasse which threatened the progress of the family.

This type of experience is, unfortunately, not uncommon for immigrant families in this country. Sometimes it does seem that even when schools do their best not to stereotype children, there may be a gulf between the parents and teachers which is quite hard to bridge. We are often involved in trying to help or advise on this sort of issue. If two parties are starting to get angry with each other, it is probably best that they meet to negotiate rather than blame each other at a distance. Equally, blaming Tony – or even his absent father – was not going to help. It was useful to acknowledge how very disappointed the family felt. Even though the mother's and grandmother's recollections of the West Indies might not be valid these days, their views on how best to manage children deserved to be treated with respect.

In this case the clinic was able to arrange for the mother and grandmother to meet some of the school teachers, and to discuss how to get Tony extra educational help. The school then realised that the family wanted Tony to do well and were willing to co-operate on educational goals. Once the atmosphere of mutual misunderstanding and blame decreased, it was much easier to start to provide Tony with the help and support he needed. Tony did respond well to the encouragement he received and got on much better at school. In turn, the tension at home also eased considerably.

Asian families, in particular, commonly wish to uphold their original cultural values. This is sometimes difficult when faced with the generation who have grown up almost entirely in modern Britain.

Raina was 16 and had been referred by her doctor because of headaches. She came from a Muslim family originally from Pakistan and was the youngest of two, having an older brother who was now doing well at university. Her father's business was quite successful, but he had to work long hours and was often away on trips abroad. Her mother had worries about her own health and tended to stay at home, looking after the house and the children and mixing almost exclusively with people from her own culture.

Raina was perceived by both parents as less bright than her brother. It was doubtful whether she would manage to achieve A levels let alone a university place, although she had stayed on at school to try to improve her GCSE grades which had been a disappointment to all. Raina had always been a rather quiet girl, but was becoming more and more moody and uncommunicative. Her parents were beginning to consider arranging a marriage sooner rather than later for Raina and had started discussing this with relatives back in Pakistan. They thought that Raina had accepted this. But now she seemed to be causing whatever difficulties she could. The topic was rarely discussed calmly within the family. Her mother was inclined to think Raina was still too young and immature, and she wanted to keep her at home with her a little longer. Her father tended to get angry and would remark that Raina obviously wasn't good enough for anything else. When her brother was at home he was quite protective towards his mother and sister, but thought that on the whole his father was right.

The GP had obviously thought that Raina's headaches were due to stress, and there certainly was conflict within the family about Raina's future. Raina's mother and father were quite ready to accept that there could be an emotional cause and to discuss the issue with us at least once. They knew that British therapists could not really understand how strongly they felt that an arranged marriage was best for their daughter, and might even disagree with their aims. We proceeded cautiously and addressed the issue as being one that needed discussion rather than sudden resolution. At the same time it seemed fair to point out not only that each member of the family had rather different views, but that Raina would have had friends with different expectations at school, even if she had not felt confident enough to discuss this at home. The family did attend for two more sessions, and the headaches improved but we did not hear the eventual outcome.

We hoped to encourage the family to consider a wider range of options for Raina and to help them communicate sufficiently well so that all members could be reasonably happy with the result.

Some families from abroad only get involved with us if one of the children does something very serious such as taking an overdose.

Susie, 15, had swallowed ten paracetamol tablets, but had then thought better of it and told her parents, who had sent for an ambulance. She was admitted overnight to a paediatric ward and our staff saw her with her parents the next day.

Susie was the only daughter of Chinese parents who were both professionals working hard to establish themselves – her father was a doctor and her mother a nurse. Their early lives had not been easy. They had been in this country for 18 years. Most of their relatives lived in Hong Kong still, and they had little contact with the Chinese community in London. They lived in a prosperous suburb of South London and their daughter attended a private girls' school, where she had done quite well academically and had several friends.

However, recently there had been tension at home because Susie's work had deteriorated according to her school, and her parents did not think she was studying hard enough for the exams which were coming up. She often asked, but was usually refused, permission to go out in the evenings with friends, and she was spending a lot of time in her room listening to what her parents thought was awful pop music. Her plans for the future seemed unrealistic to her parents – she wanted to be a vet, yet was not studying.

That a child should even have contemplated suicide is a source of shock and shame, and Susie's parents were clearly very taken aback. They felt they had given Susie everything she could possible want – even a pony – and yet she seemed to be behaving so differently from the way they had when they were young. She didn't seem to realise that you had to work for privileges. Susie's attempted suicide seemed to undermine her parents' achievements in this country. They were considering drastic measures such as sending Susie to boarding school or to relatives elsewhere.

The tension eased a bit after the initial airing of extreme feeling and Susie's voice was able to be heard. Susie had felt quite isolated as the only Chinese girl in her class and as an only child. It was not so much that she was overtly bullied, but that the other girls tended to go round in groups and leave her out. This had become even more marked as her parents would not let her go out. If she concentrated on her work and did well she was criticised for being a swot. She knew her parents wanted her to do well, but hadn't felt able to tell them her problems. Her parents talked about the difficulties of being in a different country, and how they too had experienced some of the problems which Susie was now, for the first time, beginning to tell them. The parents decided to spend more time with Susie and to discuss with her what would be reasonable in terms of her going out and doing homework. Susie clearly became much happier and more confident after a few family discussion sessions, and the parents were pleased to find out how they could help their daughter.

For all of these families, as with many British ones, the children's perceived failure lay first in the sphere of education. As the parents rebuked or nagged their children, things got worse, and family relationships deteriorated as well. The parents were very aware how they had had to struggle to achieve what they had, and it might seem to them that the child in the modern West had an easy life compared to their own childhood. However, it is the children who are particularly vulnerable to the potentially conflicting demands of two cultures. They may find it hard to discuss their difficulties, for fear of them being considered trivial by their parents.

Talking things over with a school is also more difficult for parents from abroad, because there is bound to be a lack of shared experience. Different ideas about the role of the school can lead to misunderstandings between parents and teachers, with each side reluctant to approach the other.

Usually these sorts of difficulty can be sorted out without professional help, before they get to extremes. If professional help is necessary, then it may be worth asking if someone is available who has a similar cultural background, so that they will understand more of the issues from personal experience.

10

INSTEAD OF GRIEF?

"Light griefs speak, the rest are dumb."
  Seneca

"New grief awakens the old."
  Thomas Fuller

Our modern society has reduced the amount of early and untimely death, but has also reduced mourning rituals, so that people are both unaccustomed to bereavement and unsure of how to deal with it. In clinical practice, an earlier unresolved grief can contribute to the difficulties of a current problem. Sometimes a new stress brings out memories of an old one. Sometimes the failure to overcome a challenging situation seem related to an earlier bereavement.

A child may be closely involved with this process of coming to terms with a loss, albeit unknowingly. A birth, in Nature's terms, compensates for a death, and usually brings new hope to a family. And sometimes a child is very closely identified with the lost person, which can be a source both of comfort and anxiety. This may particularly

be the case when a child has died, even one in an earlier
generation.

*Ian, two and three-quarters, attended the assessment
interview with his grandmother, Mrs Elizabeth Harvey and
his mother Ms Christine Harvey. The apparent problem
was one of "soiling", that is to say, Ian sometimes made
his "poos" in his pants or on the floor. He occasionally
went for days without passing a bowel motion. His mother
and grandmother said that they had tried "everything" –
but actually it turned out to be only negative things such
as smacking and telling him off.*

*Although Ian had actually had periods of "cleanness",
did sometimes use the toilet appropriately, and was still
very young, the grandmother especially seemed
despondent. It turned out that she herself had started to
"train" Ian from the age of six weeks, and did get
"cleanness" and "dryness" by 18 months. Relapses since
were not apparently related to any particular events or
stresses. Both the mother and grandmother felt that
achieving "cleanness" again soon was important because
Ian was about to start nursery school.*

*Ian's birth had presented no particular physical problems.
However, his parents had split up at this time and Ms
Harvey had moved back to her parents' home. As a result,
she had become quite depressed, and Ian's grandmother
had taken over most of the early care. When Ian was a few
months old his mother returned to work but continued to*

live with her parents.

The two women still shared the care of Ian now, although the mother had her own flat and a new boyfriend.

Ian was described by both women as being immature. For instance, he "wanted to cuddle", and did not like being left at the playgroup. He was also described as a "great charmer", especially with adults, but was not yet very friendly with other children.

It emerged that his mother's grandmother had died the previous year. She also had been very close to Ian and used to mind him at times. Indeed, one of the problems seemed to be that Ian "did not accept she was dead". Even more interestingly, both the great-grandmother and the grandmother had seen Ian as a replacement for Angus, Ms Harvey's younger brother, who had died at the age of four.

In the interview we observed that Ian was an attractive little boy who was shy at first, but became very responsive later. His speech was very good, with many adult "turns of phrase".

It was difficult to know which of the two women to address as the major carer, and they denied any disagreements over management. Difficult areas (such as the father situation, and the pattern of Ian's future care) were avoided. The grandmother was, rather indirectly, quite critical of both her daughter and her grandson, and she would not agree with the suggestion that soiling at the age of two was acceptable and developmentally normal.

In general "soiling" at this age is not considered anything more than a stage in the gaining of bowel control, even though it might be a little inconvenient from time to time. We wondered whether the two major carers had focused on this problem as being one which they could agree on. Possibly it helped to avoid the serious issues of Ian's past and future parenting.

There were also potential drawbacks if Ian did become "clean". Although the grandmother appeared to be complaining the most, and to be trying to push Ian into precocious achievement all round, she had the most to lose if he did become more competent and could go to nursery school. He would probably leave her home altogether.

The two bereavements mentioned by the family seemed very relevant to the situation. Firstly, the very recent death of the great-grandmother, Ian's "non-acceptance" of this, and additional symptoms of insecurity, seemed to be regarded as inappropriate by his grandmother. This attitude suggests that she herself found it difficult to grieve because she regarded such emotions as "childish".

Then Ian was openly acknowledged to be a replacement child for a dead uncle. His mother and grandmother would probably become more anxious as he neared the age of four, when his uncle died. It seemed that his grandmother would "lose" him anyway if he moved away with his mother. Although this was never explored, it is possible that the grandmother's pressure on Ian to succeed was to try and get him beyond the risky age of four as soon as possible, even if only in his achievements and behaviour.

Much of this is speculation of course, but as the family found the initial interview supportive, they did return and were helped towards their own solutions, without us having to be confrontational about our views of what was "normal". Ian's "soiling" improved very rapidly. At the same time the mother's boyfriend began to take a positive part in helping to care for the child.

Carole was two when her parents brought her to the clinic because of sleeping difficulties. The pattern was much like that of a baby and she had "never slept as much as expected". The parents reported that Carole refused to go to bed until they did, would still only settle if given a bottle of milk, insisted on being in their bed, and then slept for only short periods at a time. She was generally upset when she woke up. During the day she was active and demanding. The parents had been to their GP and health visitor but medication had not worked and they had not found advice to "be firmer" at all helpful.

Carole was immature in other ways – she was a poor eater, always wanting baby foods and milk, and her speech was a little delayed, probably due to a hearing problem – she had recently had grommets inserted. Toilet training was under way and was not a concern for her parents. She was a moody little girl who screamed when thwarted, and was sick if she cried for a long time. There were two other children – an older brother whom she seemed to dislike, and a new baby towards whom she behaved very lovingly.

It turned out that six years earlier another child, James, had died of lead poisoning aged three, because of eating lead-based paint. The parents had separated for a while after this, but were now very committed to each other. They remarked how similar Carole was to James. She had been a wanted baby and her mother had loved her from the start, but her father had been wary of getting emotionally close at first.

There were some differences apparent in the way the parents appraised the situation. Carole's mother, who now had another baby to care for, seemed most stressed by the poor sleep pattern, and was very worried that Carole might become so demanding as to be uncontrollable. The father was rather less concerned, and preferred Carole to sleep with them so that they would know she was safe.

Carole was evidently failing to "act her age" in a number of ways, yet while this was upsetting the parents, their attitudes and behaviour showed how mixed their feelings were. Carole's birth had helped to unite the couple again after the death of an older child, whom she was said to resemble. A high degree of protectiveness and indulgence is understandable in such a situation. However, as it continued it was increasingly inappropriate for her age.

On the one hand, there was now another baby, so that Carole's demands were clearly seen, at least by her mother, as excessive. On the other hand, Carole was approaching the age at which her brother had died. Straightforward "advice" had failed before with this family, so it was important to be sensitive to the speed at which the parents could move things along, when at the back of their minds all the time was their distress and probable guilt about the death of an older child.

As some degree of separation would be age-appropriate, likely to benefit Carole directly, and relieve some of the mother's stress, we suggested nursery or play-group for a few hours a week at least. This seems an obvious suggestion, but the parents may have needed professional "permission" to let their daughter out of their sight without feeling guilty. This was the first step. As a follow-up we arranged for a community psychiatric nurse to visit the family regularly at home for a few months, to discuss with them practical steps they could take to improve matters, while also acknowledging their natural anxieties.

Although the death of a child is one of the most difficult traumas to deal with, the death of an important adult figure is more commonly connected with family troubles. Sometimes this death can have occurred many years previously, as with the case below.

Peter, aged nine, was referred by his primary school head teacher because of difficult behaviour and what they described as underlying unhappiness. When he attended with his mother, Ms Ryan, it was observed that they were both very neatly dressed and sat tensely and anxiously. Ms Ryan said she had been surprised about there being problems at school, as she thought Peter liked it. But she was concerned if Peter was not getting on with his work. He mostly seemed to be cheerful and got on well with other children. However, he was a perfectionist and very conscientious. Ms Ryan had no worries about Peter's behaviour at home, where he was described as "active", enjoying games, Lego, football, drawing and reading. He had had no previous problems. Indeed, his early development was advanced if anything, as he spoke and walked very early and was reading by three and a half.

Ms Ryan had been brought up locally, the youngest of four children. Her father had died when she was 13 years old, and she cried as she told us that she had been very close to her father and still had not got over his death. She said it felt like "I died too." Until then she had been in the top stream at her school, but afterwards her school work fell apart, and she left school without passing any exams.

Her mother re-married about this time and Ms Ryan left home as she felt unwanted. She had a relationship with a student teacher, and became pregnant. This relationship ended when Peter was about 10 months old. The reasons for this were not clear; she said she felt she and Peter got on better alone.

Ms Ryan returned to college when Peter was at nursery and now had a good job as an administrative assistant and was planning to buy a house in the suburbs. She enjoyed her work but had no social life outside her own family.

She said Peter was like his grandfather in both looks and intelligence.

There was a kind of pervasive sadness about this rather isolated pair. While the mother was aware of her continued grief for her father, she had not previously considered this to be a problem, and did not realise that it might also be affecting her son's life. It was the school who noticed the boy's unhappiness and wondered if it was adversely affecting his behaviour and work. Peter's "resemblance" to his grandfather was an important comfort to his mother, but not an appropriate role for a growing boy. He also seemed to have to stand in for a male partner, as his father had been rapidly dispensed with. Perhaps it was partly because her mother had moved on so soon after widowhood that Ms Ryan felt it was up to her to keep alive the memory of her father. However, by this time the whole thing seemed chronic and dysfunctional. While the little Peter had flourished developmentally from close attention, he was now beginning to fail when having to assume an adult role.

We discussed with Ms Ryan what she could do to encourage more appropriate peer and adult male contacts for her son, and to consider how she could meet her own needs. A few sessions were held jointly with the mother and son. Then, as the boy seemed relieved that others were involved, and began to develop his own social life more happily, his mother took up the offer of counselling from a psychiatric social worker.

In this case a parental death in the previous generation was the source of problems. However, a parent's death when the children are still young can also cause immediate and continuing difficulties.

Neil had not been to school for over a term. He had been found by police playing around in a derelict shop. He was brought to the clinic by his mother. She had been very shocked, and her main concern was that Neil was failing to fulfil his potential at school.

Mrs Clements was 56, and worked as a secretary in her brother's building firm. She had three children. The oldest, Lizzie, was 19 and had recently moved away from home. Then came Neil, aged 14, and there was a younger boy, Donald.

Mr Clements had died five years previously of cancer. He had been a very industrious man with many interests. He died at home. The children had been sent away for the weekend.

As the family discussed this event with us, Neil said that he couldn't remember his mother crying, and that surprised him. Mrs Clements said it had been her duty to carry on regardless for the sake of the children. Neil said that he did not have a strong memory of his father and could not recall happy times with him, but he missed him. He thought that his mother suffered more than he did but couldn't show it. Mother and son agreed that until the father died the family lived a perfectly happy life with all the children doing well.

Now, however, there were lots of family arguments. A typical scene was that his mother argued with him, his sister came to his defence, and then his mother and sister argued – and finally he would get the blame.

Mrs Clements complained that her daughter had failed to live up to her potential. She could have done better at school and secured a better job. She was frightened that the same fate would befall Neil. Neil agreed he fought with his brother, but thought that was normal. He could "cope" with his sister. What he worried about was his mother. Mrs Clements described how she and Neil rowed quite often. She found him difficult to control.

Mrs Clements rarely went out and didn't have any close friends. She admitted she regretted much in her life, and it came over strongly that she felt unfulfilled.

There was obviously a lot of unresolved grief in this family, with the mother soldiering on and farming out responsibility or putting things down to fate. She put a lot of pressure on the children for not succeeding in the way she wanted. Unfortunately this was done in such a negative way it was counter-productive. Mrs Clements had the effect of making one very tired – nothing positive was ever taken up.

Neil was indeed a very bright boy, in touch with his feelings and able to express them. His truancy seemed to have a self-destructive tinge to it, as he knew it was not in his own best interests. The therapist thought that the family arguments, to which Neil contributed, were probably their way of expressing the pain of grief, without really communicating about, or coming to terms with, the bereavement.

Another bright child beginning to go off the rails academically ... and a focus of blame and dissent at home. Mrs Clements must have felt that simply nothing was going right for her since the illness and death of her husband, and that now her children were letting her down too. Again this mother was able to make a disappointing comparison – her son had been happy and bright before, but now he was difficult and ruining his educational chances.

In a way, the child has done his family a favour. His difficulties were so bad that they ensured the whole family got help. This mother, committed to "soldiering on" like many others, might have been reluctant to seek help only for herself. We offered the opportunity of further family discussions, to help the family come to terms with their grief and "move on", and to help Mrs Clements become more positive.

11

NOT "MINE"

"A wolf's whelp had been fostered till, one day,/Grown strong, it tore its master's life away."
  Sadi

"The hedge-sparrow fed the cuckoo so long/That it had its head bit off by its young."
  Shakespeare, *Lear*

ADOPTIVE AND FOSTER PARENTS

King Lear again – that famous disappointed, not to say embittered, parent tells the tale of the cuckoo. Although not a real member of the family, having been deposited in a sparrow's nest by his lazy and cunning parent, the cuckoo is extremely well cared for by the sparrow, only to bite his head off later. Other proverbs and fables give similar warnings about how people care for wolf cubs, lion cubs, even snakes and vipers, but then suffer for their kindness.

Many would-be adoptive and foster parents have tried to have a child of their own, a long process marked by hopes and disappointments. The quest for a "cure" for infertility is similar, with investigations and raised hopes – hopes that are all too easily dashed again.

As the parents' desire to care for a child remains strong, they decide, sometimes with reluctance on the part of one partner, to adopt. Adoption also turns out to be far from simple. There are interviews and questions, the local authorities and charities have no young babies for childless couples. Prospective parents may not be deemed suitable to be put on a waiting list, and if they are, it may be for a handicapped or older child.

Each step is one further away from the original hope of having one's own child. And yet part of the wish is also to give care and nurture to a child that is in need and who otherwise might miss a chance of happiness and fulfilment.

And so this strong altruistic urge can lead to great disappointment when, for instance, the pretty, young and affectionate child later turns out to be very difficult and challenging.

Ella was referred to the clinic by the family doctor when she was four. She had been asked to leave her rather strict and old-fashioned private nursery school because she was often aggressive to other children and constantly needed to be the centre of attention in order to behave reasonably. Her academic progress was poor.

She had been adopted at the age of ten months by her parents, who had been trying to have children for 15 years.

Her own mother had a disturbed history, having been in psychiatric hospitals from time to time, and had possibly taken drugs during the pregnancy. Little was known about the father. Her early development in her adoptive home was marked by speech delay, for which she had had therapy, and at one time there had been concerns that there might have been a hearing loss. However, by the time she was five, her speech and hearing were normal.

Ella had always been what is called "oppositional", that is to say, defiant and disobedient, not doing what she was told either at home or at school unless the boundaries were very clear. She often had temper tantrums if not immediately given her own way. Her behaviour made her unpopular with children at school and a source of great strain at home.

Ella's behaviour had become much worse after a younger boy was adopted when she was two years old. He was more placid in temperament.

Ella was blonde and pretty, but her poor attention span was evident even in the clinic, as she flitted from toy to toy and made demands on the professionals. Her behaviour contrasted with that of her younger brother, who was much more amenable.

Ella's parents were worried that she might either be showing signs of her mother's personality, or that the drugs her mother might have taken in pregnancy had affected her. They also thought that the first few months of foster care had not been of good quality. Ella's adoptive mother found it difficult to be firm with her at first, and different

113

approaches between the parents had led to arguments. However, they were now coming together with a more united approach, but Ella still remained very difficult.

It was not as simple as Ella's parents wanting a perfect child through adoption, but that the blonde baby they adopted was not living up to their high standards of behaviour and achievement. They did not wish to blame Ella or her background (and this may have added to their inability to be firm with her). They wanted to help her and not be too critical – yet the only other alternative seemed to be to blame themselves.

We decided to concentrate on the details of Ella's problems, which were indeed a "handicap", albeit of a subtle kind, and on what school and home could do specifically to help Ella make progress at her own pace. We explained that adopted children quite often show difficulties related to their early months before their permanent new family's care, and that adoption improves their lives greatly, even if it cannot completely overcome the problems. The parents were pleased at Ella's visible improvement, especially when the school was able to provide extra educational support.

Terry's foster parents were told about the Child Guidance Unit by the local authority social worker, and rang up themselves to make an appointment. At this stage they did not want to bring their foster son, as they did not want to worry him.

Terry was now 13. He had been with his foster parents for five years, and the social worker was pressing the parents to consider adoption, as she felt it would be in Terry's best interests to have a clear, permanent commitment. Unfortunately, this pressure seemed to raise the parents' anxieties about whether they had even done the right thing in the first place, as their relationship with the boy was not turning out as well as they had hoped. Terry was quite often in trouble at school, and was not achieving as well academically as his foster parents would have liked. However, being aware of this, they felt guilty, and tried not to impose their own "middle-class" hopes and values on him. This was no easy matter.

There were wider issues also. For instance, the grandparents had accepted Terry, but essentially as a foster child rather than as a full member of the family. In addition, Terry had kept in contact with his mother, and sometimes ran off to see her when it had not been formally arranged with his foster parents. Although he had been removed from home because of persistent neglect and his mother's alcoholism, he clearly still thought about her and his other brothers and sisters, and was concerned about them. He quarrelled frequently with his foster parents, challenging their authority, but afterwards could become upset and remorseful.

All this was particularly difficult for the foster mother, who felt she had invested much of herself into Terry's care, yet was being urged to greater commitment even though Terry seemed very ambivalent towards her.

Behind the intense pain of the fostering, which had not turned out as the boy, the social worker or the foster parents had hoped, there lay another disappointment – that of infertility. Just as one loss reminds you of another, so does one disappointment remind you of another disappointment, and in this case the two issues – that of failing to conceive and that of failing to be an ideal foster mother – are connected, as they both relate to motherhood.

The clinic saw the parents regularly to help them discuss both how to manage Terry's difficult behaviour in the short term, and whether to proceed with adoption. In the end, it seemed best for all to accept the imperfections, but also the benefits, of the fostering situation as it was. Terry remained very attached to his family of origin, and it seemed increasingly likely that he would wish to leave the foster-parents' home when he was 16. It was better to plan for that constructively, rather than to let a situation of mutual rejection develop.

Anna,14, was admitted for observation to the hospital after having taken an overdose of paracetamol tablets. It seemed she had not so much wanted to kill herself as to blank out the feelings of emotional pain and shame she felt after a boy had had sex with her at a party. Her parents, who were fairly recently separated, came together to discuss this crisis in their family.

The couple, who were successful professionals, had adopted two unrelated girls at young ages. The girls had until then, by and large, lived up to their parents' expectations, being attractive-looking and achieving well at school. Recently the parents' own relationship had deteriorated, and the father had moved out to live with his girlfriend.

Mostly, this was presented politely and articulately, as an unfortunate occurrence, but one that could be achieved with little distress. However, negative feelings certainly leaked out. The father's main complaint was how difficult and uncooperative his adoptive daughter Anna was with him. This seemed to be connected with the fact that in his own childhood he had had a very unhappy relationship with his parents. He had hoped in some way to avoid this, by not having children of his own "blood" .

As the girls moved into adolescence, of course they began to think of their own abilities to enjoy sex and have babies. Was Anna's early experimentation, which she denied having co-operated with, seen as a challenge by her parents not only to their thin veneer of "happy family" but also to their own "failure" to have children? Was the father's move away from the family connected to this?

A "parasuicide" act reveals a great deal of distress within a family, distress which they might generally prefer to ignore or keep quiet about. Some families prefer to retreat and not take up therapy at this point. However, this family acknowledged a range of difficulties and came together for therapy on several occasions. Of course, it did not turn into the "perfect" family, but nevertheless all members of the family found that they could communicate and negotiate their way better through the current difficult situation.

Again, many of the participants in the scenario had been disappointed – the mother in the failure of the adoption to result in a happy marriage and contented children, the father because his adopted daughter had turned against him, and the girl, who found that her father was expecting her emotional support for his misdeeds rather than vice versa.

STEP-PARENTS

Being a step-parent (or living with a partner who has children) is now very common. In the past, as shown in fairy tales by the Brothers Grimm and Charles Perrault, the step-mother was seen as a universally wicked figure, even though, as in *Snow White* or *Cinderella*, the natural mother had died and so the father had not been lured away. A "happy ending" for the heroine involves not only the attainment of a handsome prince, but the intense dis-comfiture of the step-mother.

These days the step-father is regarded with some suspicion. If he apparently abandoned his own children what does that imply? Is he going to stay and be a father-figure with some authority? And even – has he only joined the family to gratify his sexual urges with the children, whether girls or boys?

Many step-parents are likely to enter into the situation with some reservations, realising that there may be difficulties. But they may well assume that with the love they have for their new partner and a reasonable approach, all will be well. Often there is real desire to have a constructive and important relationship with the children, especially if the "real" equivalent parent is no longer available through death or desertion.

Yet as the fairy tales reveal, emotions and attitudes are not entirely rational. The "step-children" may be hostile and seem to be trying to break up the new couple despite the best and most well-intentioned efforts of the newcomer.

Jake, aged 12, was referred to the clinic by the Education Welfare Officer. His mother, step-father and younger brother were also present at the interview.

Jake was reported to be persistently untruthful. For example, his parents were sure he had stolen £25 from their bedroom, but he denied it. Since starting secondary school he had frequently played truant. Jake often went missing from home for short periods of time and had returned to his father on a number of occasions. The parents also felt that Jake was at risk of becoming delinquent, as he kept "bad" company, and had once been brought home by the police, having been caught trespassing on the roof of a warehouse. Jake seemed to be generally unhappy at school and his parents wondered if he was being victimised. Jake had also started wetting the bed since his step-father had joined the family.

One source of inter-parental conflict was that Jake had always been a fussy eater, and had always been allowed to eat what he liked when he liked. His step-father did not approve of this and insisted on "proper meals".

On the good side, Jake was very patient with his younger sibling, and very helpful in the home and in the step-father's workshop. He was also generous, affectionate and sensitive. His mother said, "He's beautiful." He continued to get on well with his older brothers, who had remained with his father and whom he saw weekly.

Jake was the third of four children by his mother's first marriage. He had been a wanted and contented child. The marriage had deteriorated with the father being away from home a lot as an insurance salesman, and mother running a catering business. When they had separated two years previously the two older children stayed with the father, and the two younger ones went to live with the mother. The current couple had been living together for 16 months and the step-father had three children by a previous marriage, whom he saw regularly.

The step-father was anxious, clearly angry and hurt, yet also showing sympathy and care for Jake and his problems. He said he shed tears about his efforts to get on with Jake and felt rejected by Jake's bad behaviour. The couple feared that his behaviour might cause a rift between them and were determined to prevent this.

The therapist thought that Jake seemed unhappy and anxious, and was probably afraid of his step-father. The step-father's intense efforts to get on top of the situation seemed to be partly related to his guilt about having left his own children and trying to ensure things went better this time around. There was thus a vicious circle.

As they discussed their worries more, the mood of the family lightened a bit, and they were able to consider going to the school together to try to tackle the problem of non-attendance.

This step-father was in the classic position of trying to do even better, both than he had managed before, and than the "real" father. He was therefore deeply upset when one of the children in his new family did not overtly reject him but seemed to challenge his effective authority. Fortunately this couple recognised that there was a problem and sought help.

A step-parent may, of course, be disappointed for similar reasons to an "ordinary" parent, but the emotions aroused may be complicated by their position ...

Stewart, aged 13, was referred to the Child Guidance Unit by his school because his work was poor and he seemed to be easily victimised.

121

His mother had died when he was two years old and his father had re-married fairly quickly. His step-mother had willingly taken on the two – husband and step-son – and had put a great deal of effort into ensuring Stewart had lots of loving care and attention.

This had been successful to the degree that Stewart was very pleasant in manner and was in the "grammar stream" of his rather old-fashioned school. However, as Stewart was getting older, and she did not have younger children of her own, the step-mother was now hoping he could become more independent so that she could develop her career. This was impeded by Stewart's mysterious failure in secondary school, and the step-mother was becoming increasingly frustrated and irritated by him. The father remained relaxed and rather distant, preferring to leave matters to his wife.

Psychological testing eventually showed that Stewart had marked learning difficulties, almost certainly of a type of in-born mental handicap. This had been masked by the excellence of the early care and coaching provided by his step-mother, but it would be impossible for him to cope with the advanced academic type of education that he was receiving.

The school did not have the facilities to deal with Stewart's difficulties, and in the end the happiest compromise for all concerned was for him to be placed in a boarding school for children with special educational needs.

It is still a common pattern for a father to leave most of the day-to-day concerns of parenting to his wife even if, as here, the children are not hers. For this step-mother, who had high standards and had more than done her bit in terms of early care, she might have been blamed for Stewart's failure when in her mind it was mainly Stewart's fault for "not trying". The diagnosis of mental handicap at least reduced these possible sources of "fault" and provided a clearer path to follow.

12

BOYS AND GIRLS

"What are little girls made of?
Sugar and spice and all things nice.
What are little boys made of?
Slugs and snails and puppy dogs' tails."
Traditional

Issues of gender and sexuality are easier to discuss in public nowadays. Yet in the emotional heat of family life, they can still be sources of great tension and be difficult to talk about, mainly because everyone is embarrassed.

For instance, is the new baby the boy or girl that was wanted? Still current in our society is the idea of the male "line" mediated by the male name. This and other values may mean that the birth of a boy is more desirable than that of a girl. In some cultures, where there are even stronger social and economic pressures, this is even more overt. It is increasingly likely that soon it will be commonplace for parents to choose the gender of their children. This may have unforeseen social consequences.

Sometimes, a girl is wanted and not a boy. One such case is described by Jean Renvoize in her book *Children in Danger*. Mrs Jones, who had a number of social and marital problems, felt very hostile towards her baby son, to the extent of actually harming him. She said, "I was terribly disappointed when they told me. I just don't like boys all that much. You can't even dress them up like you can girls."

I rarely see families where the issue is that explicit. Many parents these days try to avoid stereotyping and it is not uncommon for fairly "natural" behaviour such as little boys' enjoyment of playing with guns to be viewed as shocking and undesirable.

The following case shows again how one apparent "problem" – here a father's inability to get on with his small daughter – usually has many causes, one of which was "prejudice" about the child's sex.

Four-year-old Frances had been referred by her day nursery and attended with her father Mr Barratt, her step-mother Mrs Barratt and her six-year-old brother Bill.

Apparently, Frances was extremely active, very bad-tempered and as she got over-tired, destructive and "vicious". As a result she had no friends, adults did not like to baby-sit her and she wore down both parents' nerves. The problem was long-standing.

Frances's general health was excellent. She was very bright, demanding and needed lots of attention. A variety of techniques had been tried with her, but most had only temporary effectiveness. The parents were trying not to smack her, but gave sweets to Frances at the end of the

125

day if she had been good, and sent her to bed early if she was very naughty. However, Frances tended to get the last word – such as "I don't care" – whenever she was punished. She came for cuddles sometimes if tired, but seemed to find it difficult to relax or take a midday nap. She attended a day nursery, where she was also difficult. Indeed, the staff were quite concerned about her aggression towards other children, and whether she would be able to cope with primary school when the time came.

Her father knew little about the details of Frances's birth. In fact he said he hardly knew she was there as a small baby, as she did not cry and slept a lot. When her mother suddenly left, she was nine months old, and did not seem to recognise her father.

Helen Barratt, Frances's "real" mother, was said to be "backward", and very like Frances in personality; in other words – difficult. Since she left home she had only been in contact six times altogether, and other members of her family had not helped or been in touch either.

John Barratt had been a building foreman, but was now unemployed. His own parents had separated and he had always been closer to his father, "a Daddy's boy". It was his father he turned to after Frances's mother left. His mother had disliked him, as she had wanted a girl. However, he got on better with his mother now he was a parent himself.

Mary Barratt, the step-mother, had been with the family full-time for about the last year, and had been going out *with the father for three years before then.*

Bill, five, was said to be very quiet. At home he tended to be dominated by Frances. He still remembered his real mother a little. Significantly, he was also described as "Daddy's boy".

Frances was, curiously enough, called Angela when good and Frances when naughty. She was said not to recognise or remember her mother.

Frances was tall for her age, very active and demanding, especially to Mary. She broke the usual expectations of behaviour at the clinic by doing things such as turning on the taps and chalking on the walls. Eventually Mary, and on one occasion her father, intervened to stop her. Mary seemed to encourage her when she played, but did not attempt to calm or cuddle her, while the father interacted very little with her.

Mr Barratt was rather quiet at first, uncertain how much to say about his ex-wife. He maintained that the past was not part of Frances's problem, even though he called her "sadistic" and very like her mother. The period immediately after the desertion seemed to have been a very painful one indeed, in which he had been unable to get close to Frances and had "let her get away with things". Now, if Frances got on his nerves, he left her to Mary.

Mary seemed a sensible young woman who had contributed a lot to the family. At first she smiled when talking about Frances's misdeeds, but as the interview progressed, she showed the strain placed on her. She "wanted to know why" and had been thinking mainly of dietary causes.

At the first assessment we felt that Frances was an oppositional little girl, temperamentally very active, whose early attachments had been disrupted by her mother's desertion at the age of five months. Her father seemed to have been so upset when his wife left that he had paid very little close attention to his baby daughter. The family seemed to be coping much better since the full-time presence of the step-mother in the family, even though there were still major difficulties.

As the psychotherapist treating this case discovered, the problem within the family was a very deep-rooted one. The initial mutual attachment of this father and his baby daughter had been blighted for a number of reasons. However, their relationship seemed to continue to be poor mainly because she was a girl. This was not just because she resembled her mother, who had let them all down, but was also because it was a repetition of events which the father had experienced in his own childhood. He felt that boys were for fathers and fathers were for boys, and so he could not even begin to imagine a good relationship with his daughter.

Fortunately there were enough strengths now within this family unit for Frances to feel happier and start to settle down. Although the father did not always come, the rest of the family regularly attended sessions with the psychotherapist. As the parents were encouraged to notice Frances's good points and respond to her need for physical affection, Frances did become easier to manage both at home and at school.

Moving from gender to sexuality, we find another great issue for parents to cope with. "Teenage sex" provides good material for a tabloid headline, but despite its evident widespread occurrence, it still causes much anxiety to parents, especially those with daughters. It is not just a simple matter of sex or no sex, but that a teenage girl may seem to be behaving in a way quite contrary to her parents' aspirations, however liberal they would like to be, and they fear that she herself may regret it later, as often they have done themselves.

Julia's mother, Mrs Dale, had requested the appointment at the clinic, saying her daughter was "throwing her life away". When the parents arrived, accompanied by their daughters, 16-year-old Julia and 14-year-old Clare, Mrs Dale elaborated that Julia was often in trouble at school, was argumentative at home, and wouldn't confide in her.

She had been somewhat difficult at school for the last two years, but only over the previous six months had she become a problem at home.

The discussion came round to sex fairly quickly: Mrs Dale said, unconvincingly, that she did not mind if Julia had boyfriends. Mr Dale, on the other hand, said that it was his greatest worry that Julia was having sex and might get pregnant. It was clear that the parents found this topic a very difficult one to discuss with their daughter.

School issues were the next major worry. Julia did not seem interested in GCSEs. Again the parents' expectations were not clear. Mrs Dale said she hoped Julia might be a dancer, while Mr Dale said he would like his daughter to go to university.

Both parents were originally from working-class backgrounds, but had gone to grammar school. The mother had had both her children when under 20, and the first pregnancy had "forced" the marriage.

The interviewer thought that Julia's behaviour was resonating with the parents' own experiences of adolescence and that, as a result, they were not giving a clear message about their expectations.

Middle-class parents do often give out "double messages". They tell their children that they "just want them to be happy", but countermand this by being confused and upset if the children do not "spontaneously" choose an approved, achieving path. With the Dale family it helped to go over the parents' experiences of adolescence. Both the daughters could then hear about the dilemmas, wishes and struggles of their parents when they were young, and hear them talk about their wishes for the future. One of the things a relative outsider, such as a therapist, can do is to help put a seemingly insurmountable problem into perspective. A bit of humour does not go amiss either!

For some parents the transformation of their child to a sexually active adult is marked by even more upheavals to their hopes and expectations. It is still not easy, for instance, for parents to accept that their child may not be heterosexual. Social stigma can still be attached to this, and then there is the loss of likely grandparenthood. In some parts of this country and within some cultures, there may be even greater difficulties.

Bibi was the daughter of a well-to-do Asian family, living in London. Her father was a doctor and her mother was also a graduate. She had one older brother and a younger sister. Her early development had been unremarkable, except for aping boys' manners a bit, in a tomboyish sort of way. Nevertheless it had been possible to get her into a sari on special occasions. She was a clever child, and did very well academically at a small independent girls' school.

When she was in her mid-teens, her parents were pleased that she did not have boyfriends but went round with a group of girls. However, when she was 18 and studying for her A levels, Bibi fell in love with a girl at school who had been her friend for years.

Bibi at first felt she could not discuss this with her parents, and presented herself to a doctor saying she thought she really wanted to be a boy and could she have an operation to help. The clinic persuaded her to bring her parents in for discussion.

131

Naturally the parents were very shocked at first and blamed the other girl (also a Muslim) for being too westernised. They had not been going to arrange marriages for their children, but had hoped that they would choose acceptable partners themselves. They now had to face the fact that Bibi would probably never marry, as her attraction to women rather than men seemed to be long-standing and exclusive. They saw, however, that Bibi could achieve and be happy in other ways, and slowly became reconciled to this.

While homosexual (gay and lesbian) attachments are now more accepted and understood, the issue of the rarer "transsexuality" has often not got beyond the smutty joke stage. A primary transsexual is someone who thinks from the outset that they are in the wrong kind of body, and this is more common in boys. Usually, such a boy prefers to dress in girls' clothes and play with dolls from a very young age, but then responds to parental and peer pressure and appears to behave like a normal boy. Later, transsexuals may be apparently homosexual but not entirely satisfied. When children ask for a "sex change" some parents feel this is a kind of rejection of themselves. Others can come to construe transsexuality as an illness which may be "cured" by a sex-change operation.

Keith Martin was the second son in his family. His father was a businessman and his mother worked part-time as a secretary. *From about the age of two and a half Keith insisted he was a girl. He liked to dress up in girls' clothes. He refused to play with guns and soldiers, saying those were "boys' things to do". When he was at nursery school he would only play with the girls. His parents at first found it amusing when he dressed up in girls' clothes, but later discouraged it, although they did argue about whether this was cruel.*

When Keith started main school he stopped talking about "being a girl", to avoid teasing. However, he secretly put on his mother's clothes when the family was out.

At secondary school Keith was at first rather shy, withdrawn and bookish, avoiding sports when he could. At puberty he realised he was sexually attracted to other boys and began a phase of over-compensation to disguise this. He joined a motorcycle gang, began to smoke, take drugs and commit minor delinquencies.

This was a time of considerable family tension, and his father left home, partly because of rows over how to deal with Keith's difficult behaviour.

At 17, after having taken an overdose, Keith confided in his GP and was referred to a specialist service. There, Keith began to express again his view that he would rather go through life as a female. His mother was invited to attend the specialist clinic and was rather surprised to hear Keith's plan, but as it was evidently making him happier she accepted it. He began to "cross-dress" permanently and to take female hormones.

Parents cannot, of course, be prepared for all eventualities, especially rare ones. Sometimes, what happens to children can be put down to chance, sometimes it was perhaps foreseeable, at others the teenager seems to have picked on the one thing most likely to upset their parents. Despite all their surprise and admitted disappointment, however, parents are often able to alter their views of what is acceptable and move on to a different kind of relationship with their adult children.

13

THE LAST STRAW

"It is the last straw that breaks the camel's back."
  Proverb

"Misfortunes never come single."
  Addison

If a child – particularly one with a long history of problems – is being difficult at a time when there are also external stresses on the family, it can lead to a "last straw" situation and the family seek help.

  When family tension is so high it is usually very difficult to see the wood for the trees. Often the child's behaviour is not actually an intentional additional irritant, but may be a response to the stresses facing the whole family.

  In the clinic we usually let the family relax by getting a lot off their chest before rushing in with advice. This may take quite a while, but it is very important, as parents in this situation commonly feel that they have already exhausted all possible avenues. They think that other people are only going to blame them or make impossible demands on them.

135

Alan was nine years old when he came to the Child Guidance Unit, accompanied by his mother and small brother Tom, aged three. His mother explained that she was now at the end of her tether because of Alan's bad behaviour. She said that since the birth of his brother he had become sullen and uncommunicative. He cried a lot and this exasperated his mother. He was jealous of his little brother and constantly complained that he was not treated in the same way. Alan had also developed eczema on his skin for the last three years, which was itchy and led to painful cracks. He was being treated at the hospital, but was often difficult about putting on the cream. This led to further arguments between mother and son, as did Alan's continued scratching, which was making his skin worse.

What precipitated the attendance, however, was pressure from the school. Alan's academic progress, especially in reading and writing, was deteriorating. The school report, which the mother brought along, said that Alan could not concentrate, never got on with his work and "seemed to be in a world of his own". His teacher thought that he was quite able enough to be doing better than this.

Alan's mother did not say very much about his father except that the parents had divorced six years ago and the father did make occasional contact. She had a reasonably good relationship with the father of the younger boy, but saw herself primarily as a single parent, with nearly all the responsibilities of finance and of childcare falling on her shoulders.

In earlier years, things had not been so bad, and Alan had not had any problems with development or adjustment. Now, however, Alan's mother found it almost impossible not to be highly critical of him. Even in the first interview we observed that Alan withdrew further into himself when his mother made any verbal attack, and that this made his mother even more irritated with him.

The interviewer thought that Alan had clearly been upset by his parents' marriage break-up and was jealous of the new younger brother from a different relationship, who seemed to him to be getting more attention from his parents. Meanwhile, his mother's extreme negativity towards him was making things even worse. Somehow he was not living up to her expectations, and he was also getting blamed for his father's lack of support.

We always try to look at a situation as a whole and not blame any one person in a family. Simple advice and explanation seemed unlikely to relieve anything, as the mother was upset and fixed in her allocation of the blame.

The situation was clearly one of high "Expressed Emotion", where the parent is both very involved with their child, and yet also intensely critical. In the short term, "blaming" a particular individual allows others to escape scrutiny, including oneself. But if your own child is the focus, you can't just walk away from the difficulty for ever. The team's approach in this case was to offer quite long-term regular supportive counselling to the mother on her own, to allow her to air her problems and even begin to look at how some of her past experiences with her own family and relationships were affecting the present ones. Meanwhile we got in touch with the school, both to reassure them that we were taking the whole issue seriously and to discuss with them what sort of extra help, either from them or from us, might most benefit Alan. We also discussed with Alan's mother how his father could be more positively involved, even though she still felt considerable resentment.

Gradually, Alan's mother began to relax, and she was able to acknowledge a mixture of good and bad in Alan as well as in herself and other family members. As things started to improve, she was even able to see the humorous side of things. Alan became more communicative and was able to take part in family discussions in a more positive way. He also became more confident and successful at school, and his mother was pleased with his progress.

David, ten, was brought to the clinic because his father was extremely concerned about his lack of educational progress. Mr Ellison was almost in tears as he spoke of David's educational difficulties and then of the unhappy family events.

David was said not to remember words unless there was a picture association. At first, professionals had apparently not accepted that there was a problem, as David seemed quite intelligent. But now, although the school realised there was a specific academic difficulty and had offered extra help, David was still making little progress. It was for this reason that Mr Ellison had been advised by the school to seek outside help.

David's birth and early developmental milestones were normal, but the recent family history had been a stormy one. Both his parents had been married before and had children by those relationships, so that David had one half-sister and three half-brothers.

Initially this family group had all lived happily together, until the previous year, when the mother had become depressed. She went on holiday to Turkey and then returned to stay there, apparently permanently, with a man she met while on holiday. This had, not surprisingly, caused a great shock to the family. Her older daughter, 14, ran away from home and was currently living with a school friend. She was truanting and behaving promiscuously. Mr Ellison's two older children, both in their twenties, had left home in a more organised way, but were now living in America near their mother's family. In addition, Mr Ellison's business was in a state of near collapse, partly because of the mother's reckless spending before she left for Turkey.

Mr Ellison was inclined to blame his wife and perhaps the school, but was feeling so distressed and without support himself that he simply did not know how to cope with another set of problems such as David's lack of educational progress. In the interview David seemed fidgety and could not settle. He talked about his likes and dislikes but was reluctant to discuss his mother at all.

In the face of so much confusion and distress, the team once again decided to take matters slowly, and offer Mr Ellison the time and space to sort things out with a male counsellor. He could then begin to make his own decisions. David was assessed further by an educational psychologist and was also offered remedial help by the clinic teacher. He began to make slow progress. In the end, Mr Ellison began to put his life back together, but the best arrangement seemed to be for David to go to boarding school. A suitable school was found for him which could both cope with his specific educational difficulties (a form of dyslexia) and provide the stability that he needed.

Mr and Mrs Taylor were in a state of desperation when they brought their daughters Ingrid, seven, and Polly, four, to the hospital clinic. Although Polly had epilepsy and needed a great deal of care and attention, she was not seen as "the problem". Ingrid, on the other hand, had become more and more difficult since her sister's birth. At home she was defiant and would not do what she was told. For instance, in the mornings she fussed and delayed so much about getting washed and dressed that they were nearly always late. At school she was getting into trouble because, although she seemed an able and articulate child, her reading was poor and she dawdled over all her work.

Mrs Taylor had a good job before the children were born, working as an office administrator. Now, however, she was working as the secretary for the school at which both her children attended, partly in order to be able to keep an eye on Polly. The job in itself had become very stressful with all the new government reforms, and she was the kind of person who tended to take work home to get it finished properly. Ingrid's misbehaviour and failures at school therefore intruded into her working life as well.

The father was able to distance himself more from the problem, but was no better able to get Ingrid to obey him, and was having work problems of his own. His company, where he was a manager, had recently been taken over, and he thought it was very likely that there would be redundancies. He had begun to feel that the jobs would go, not to the most able, but to those most prepared to toe the party line.

In most other ways the family was successful and reasonably content, being on good terms with grandparents, and having friends and social organisational links with their suburban community, where they were involved with local charitable works.

It seemed to these parents that they had done a lot for both their children and their community, but now, as problems were beginning to pile up, Ingrid, who had no obvious "problems" as her sister did, was letting them down.

The clinic team thought that Ingrid was operating as a sort of "lightning conductor" for family problems. All the other family members had their own difficulties but hers seemed to be the final focus. Ingrid had been referred for very similar reasons before. Mr and Mrs Taylor had previously found advice and support helpful, and it was not clear why the situation had deteriorated again so quickly.

Even though the immediate worries and Ingrid's difficult behaviour improved rapidly, we offered further exploratory interviews to the couple alone. These did turn out to be illuminating and helpful, so that next time these parents might be able to stand back a bit and say, "Although it feels like it, we know the situation is not just our daughter's fault – what can we all do to improve things?"

Luckily, in all of these cases, although the camel (the parents) was on its knees, it realised that the last straw was just a straw – in other words an issue that, if all else were equal, could have been borne. It's often difficult to see this except in hindsight – when the whole load has been lightened, to continue the metaphor. Or perhaps the poor camel will be able to pick up its burden again if it has the equivalent of a rest and a drink. All the family members will benefit from encouragement, in order to help break the self-defeating vicious circle of blame and hopelessness.

For parents reading this who may recognise this scenario, my advice would be to unburden yourselves within the family, to friends or your doctor, or to the child's school by telling them your experiences and feelings. Of course it can be a bit embarrassing, but you will find people are often ready to listen and they may have practical help to offer. Try and stand back a bit. Don't blame yourself, but listen for constructive suggestions and accept help when it is offered. You may not need specific advice on how to improve your child's reading or behaviour, so much as a little spare coping capacity. Then, as the tension eases, at least some of your child's problems are likely to diminish, and you will be in a better frame of mind to sort things out systematically.

14

THE PERFECT FAMILY

"He that hath wife and children hath given hostages to fortune."
  Francis Bacon

Each society has its own notion of an ideal family, and ours is still of father, mother and "two point four" children, doing well and living in reasonable harmony. While we ourselves struggle with this, or see quite successful alternative arrangements, some families appear to embody the ideal. Sometimes this "happy family" is a complete facade, hiding a family secret of which some at least are conscious – such as parental alcoholism, or infidelity. Sometimes the parental perfectionism gets taken to an extreme by the children, so that it becomes a failure or even a disgrace.

  Children referred to the clinic with obsessional behaviour or with symptoms of anorexia often come from apparently normal if not "super-normal" families. It is often hard to work out quite what has gone wrong, while the perfectionistic stubbornness of the child defeats the parents and sometimes the therapists as well.

Davina was 13, the daughter of two university lecturers. She was a pretty, slender girl with long blonde hair which fell over her face as she slumped forward in a dejected way. She sat between her parents, who reached out to pat her anxiously from time to time.

It only slowly emerged what the difficulties were, as Davina's parents, Mr and Mrs Freeman, were not sure if they were sufficiently serious to be bothering us with, and they also did not want to upset their daughter.

For the past 18 months Davina had developed "obsessions", as she called them. These took two main forms. Firstly, her thoughts: she said she "wished" something awful would happen. Then she would have to go to her mother and seek repeated reassurance that what she "wished" was not going to happen. She would not go to her father usually, as he was not very sympathetic. Her mother, however, always reassured her, as Davina's anxieties reminded her of some she had had herself in the past.

The other problem was that Davina's preparations for going to bed were getting longer and longer. Everything had to be done in the right order, sometimes repeated several times, and if she thought a "bad thought" on the way, sometimes she had to start the sequence all over again. Her parents had not realised quite how bad this was until they went on holiday and had to share closer quarters than usual. These "rituals" were now taking up to two hours.

There were no obvious major stresses or difficulties in

145

the family background. The father's work took him away quite a lot, but the family did not see this as a problem.

Davina's demands for reassurance and the time she spent in the bathroom were now a considerable interference in family life. Yet it seemed quite hard for these caring and intelligent parents to admit that it was wearing them down and making them angry.

After two interviews the family wrote to say they did not wish to come again. Even though they realised that Davina's symptoms were a bit troublesome, they had improved a bit, and they thought that would be sufficient. They felt that they certainly did not want Davina to become a less conscientious sort of person, as that might affect her school work.

Because the clinical assessment and intervention was brought to a rather early end by the parents, we did not get far enough to test a number of hypotheses about the family dynamics which had produced this quite abnormal and distressing pattern of symptoms in Davina. (Although the symptoms closely resembled the full-blown obsessive compulsive disorder found in adults, we often find that the symptoms can be much more fluid with children, and improve rapidly.) Being "good", quiet, conscientious and not overtly angry, were so valued by the family that an attempt to alleviate the obsessional symptoms even by discussion seemed like an unbearable intrusion. Davina's perfectionist personality therefore was largely in line with what the parents were trying to achieve, and they did not want the status quo of the family to be disturbed.

Andrea was the older of two girls. She had always done well academically at school, and also at sports, drama and her special love, ballet.

Andrea was 12 when she was first seen by the child psychiatrist. Six months before, she had developed severe headaches with vomiting, and these had been investigated by the neurologist without any specific cause being found. At about the same time as the headaches, Andrea had begun to lose weight rapidly. At first this seemed to be due to her not eating things like chocolate, in order to help prevent headaches. Later, it became clear she was trying to lose weight for its own sake. When she attended the clinic she was already very underweight.

On closer discussion it emerged that Andrea's periods had started six months before, and she viewed them with disgust. They had stopped again as she lost weight. She had a distorted body image, so that when she looked at herself in the mirror she thought she was fat even though she was actually very skinny. Her parents, her friends and her doctors had all told her she was not fat, but she was only willing to agree that she did not need to lose any more weight, not that she needed to gain some. She had also been exercising excessively, even beyond what her normal dancing and athletics regimes called for.

She was extremely faddy about her food, had become a

vegetarian, constantly counted calories, and refused to eat with the rest of the family. She had also recently become quite withdrawn and miserable.

Andrea had previously been a "model child" in her parents' eyes, and was quite a perfectionist. She had ambitions to be a dancer one day.

Her parents were prosperous and settled in their community. Her father was a stockbroker, and her mother did part-time voluntary work. The younger sister had no problems either at school or at home. No recent major family stresses or worries emerged. On the whole they seemed to be a family which avoided argument and conflict, with the mother very much taking the role of peace-maker. This tactic unfortunately was not working well with Andrea's refusal to eat.

The diagnosis was clearly anorexia nervosa, and weekly meetings were arranged with the family. The first step was to communicate the diagnosis and extreme seriousness of the situation. The next stage was to negotiate a programme for weight gain, which included setting a target weight, establishing a satisfactory rate of weight gain, establishing parental responsibility for the supervision of meals, and looking at sanctions and rewards.

At first the parents found it very hard to unite and comply with the instructions – and Andrea lost further weight. In fact, it was only when we started to arrange hospital admission that the parents realised how serious a problem it was, and they began to ensure together that she ate more.

It also helped that the dancing teacher refused to let Andrea attend her classes until she put on weight. And so, week by week, under close supervision, and objecting much of the way, Andrea began to eat better and put on weight. After several months she had attained a reasonable weight and her periods had started again. She and her family seemed not only more cheerful, but more able to have open disagreements and resolve them without catastrophe. Andrea was even beginning to look forward to teenage life.

Andrea's tale is of a classic type of anorexia nervosa, starting fairly young, almost immediately after the onset of menstruation. This condition mainly affects girls from middle-class families, and would-be dancers are very prone to it.

Parental efforts to be "kind" and cater as far as possible to all sorts of teenage whims do avoid conflict at first. But anorexia nervosa is an extremely serious condition which can be fatal. Luckily, the techniques for helping families with this problem are now quite well understood, and Andrea made good progress.

Occasionally a child may seem "perfect" to their parents but because of the self-same characteristics quite the opposite to their school and fellow-children ...

Gregory was referred by his health visitor at the age of six, as his teachers were worried about his "unusual behaviour". *Gregory was thought to be of very high intelligence; his reading and writing were much better than nearly all his class-mates'. However, he also stood out in school because he persisted in pursuing and expressing his own ideas during group activities, and would interrupt discussions and story-telling with irrelevant thoughts of his own. He did not interact much with the other children, staying mostly on his own. He even looked eccentric amongst the other children, as he was fussy about clothes and insisted on wearing a suit and tie or a uniform, unlike the others who were casually dressed.*

When we met the family it was immediately evident which of the two boys was Gregory – the one with the "short-back-and-sides" haircut dressed in white shirt, tie, waistcoat and dark suit. His older brother, Alan, was wearing a T-shirt and jeans. In the interview, Gregory tended to comment on things using long words in a rather pompous and precocious way.

Mr and Mrs Devon did not really understand what the fuss was about and thought the school was making a mountain out of a molehill. Mr Devon was self-employed and doing well. Mrs Devon helped her husband with his business. They presented a picture of a happy family who enjoyed going out together to parks and museums. Alan was of an easy-going temperament and tended to give way or cater to Gregory to avoid arguments. For instance, if the boys made a mess, it was Alan who cleared it up as Gregory would refuse. Gregory was obviously being treated as very "special" even by his brother.

After some discussion, the parents agreed that Gregory often refused to do what he was told, but they did not consider this to be very serious. The father thought that he and Alan were alike – placid and tolerant types; he thought that Gregory was a bit more like his mother – attractive, quieter, yet persistent. Mrs Devon seemed quite happy to go along with this.

We encouraged the parents to be fairer to Alan and more firm with Gregory over the usual sorts of issues like going to bed and tidying up. Our rationale was that it was not going to be helpful in the long run for Gregory to expect the sort of indulgence from everyone else that he got from his family – no matter how bright he was. He needed to learn at home that he was just a child, not a mini-adult, so that when at school he would obey the rules like everyone else.

This approach went well, and the parents reported a rapid improvement in Gregory's behaviour at home and at school. Somewhat to our surprise, after three sessions Gregory appeared dressed as casually as his brother, although we had not commented on his clothes at all!

In all of the case histories in this chapter, although the issues varied in severity, the parents were inadvertently making matters worse by keeping to their previously successful methods of lots of attention, even indulgence. They were also trying to avoid conflict and criticism, and while this is a noble aim, it can cause other problems. In all cases there were no major family stresses or losses (though the parents might have minimised them). The children's behaviours were in many ways socially desirable – they had just gone that little bit too far. This can be very difficult for parents to perceive at first, especially when their previous experience has been good. Such parents may need encouragement to be firmer with their children, and learn that this is not "nastiness" and a failure of parenthood, but one of its essential tasks.

15

WHAT NOT TO DO

It is not that easy to learn from your own mistakes. Although
you may know intellectually that an error was made, you
may be too involved to be able to reflect dispassionately.
And negative resolutions – for example not to over-eat, or
not to smoke – are among the hardest to keep.

Nevertheless, perhaps a little understanding can be gained
from considering where others may have gone wrong, and
you may begin to entertain the possibility that you have
been in a similar situation yourself.

The following list is a set of "Don'ts" which could be
derived from the preceding case histories. They are all
easier said than done ...

DON'T MAKE INVIDIOUS COMPARISONS

"It is Comparison that makes men happy or miserable."
  Thomas Fuller

Making comparisons is a very natural human trait, but it
not only causes extra misery for the parent making the

153

comparison, but also causes the child to develop or behave even less well. Sometimes the parent knows with whom they are comparing the child. Several of the families described had one "bad" child, and the rest were "good". Shane, for instance, who was a prematurely born twin, came off less well than his twin brother. Elaine, who had taken an overdose, was criticised in comparison with her younger sisters. Janine was simply less pretty and outgoing than her younger sister.

Obviously, children can also come off worse when compared with other boys and girls of the same age, whether at school (bottom of the class) or in the park (slower to walk).

Parents often compare a disappointing child to themselves at a similar age. This was true in the cases of Mark, whose dedication to rock music above school work was wrecking his chances of becoming a successful professional like his parents, and Michael, who didn't do any homework.

Other comparisons are with ideals rather than realities. For instance, a handicapped baby is disappointing partly in comparison with the expected "normal" ideal, or a child is compared unfavourably by its parents with what they imagine a baby who died might have been like.

Comparisons are inevitable, but what is really invidious is if they are always negative.

DON'T HAVE UNREASONABLE EXPECTATIONS

"Blessed is the man who expects nothing, for he shall never be disappointed."
  Pope

Some of the unreasonable expectations that turned up in the case histories were that:
– children will have the best characteristics of their parents
– kindness will in itself produce good behaviour
– giving a lot to a child will produce gratitude
– children will avoid their parents' mistakes
– children will do at least as well as their parents if not better
– telling children off makes them more obedient.

These are, unfortunately, mistaken views about the nature of children, especially if the word "always" is contained in them. Of course, some children do achieve all the above and more, and seem to confirm their parents' theories of parenthood – but the next child may be different.

However, it is possible to have expectations which are too low as well as too high. Having low, or no, expectations will not help in the day-to-day care and guidance that children need.

DON'T CRITICISE ALL THE TIME

"Speak roughly to your little boy/And beat him when he sneezes./He only does it to annoy,/Because he knows it teases."

Lewis Carroll

This is the Duchess's strange and violent lullaby to her baby in *Alice in Wonderland*. Alice gets handed the baby, and tries to be kinder, but it is too late – it has already turned into a pig – and off it goes.

Some of the parents I meet are so tense that, at the first interview, they criticise one child for the whole hour. It is fairly clear that at home also this same child is subject to lots of nagging. The child's behaviour may be, and usually is, absolutely dreadful – defiant, lying and destructive, for instance. It might seem to a parent that everything is wrong with their child and always has been, even though they love him or her tremendously. Alan's mother had begun to feel this way about him; he was miserable, failing at school and had eczema, and she even found the way he reacted to criticism very irritating and provoking.

The criticism may well be "deserved" and the desperate response of the parent understandable – but it only makes matters worse. Again, it is not occasional criticism that is the problem, but the persistent, often highly emotional kind. This kind of behaviour was discussed in the second chapter, and described as high "Expressed Emotion". It is associated with poor outcome in a number of psychiatric conditions, but parents can learn to reduce it.

DON'T PUNISH USELESSLY

"All punishment is mischief."
  Jeremy Bentham

If a parent is disappointed and annoyed by a child's actions, particularly if they are quite young, they often have a strong urge to punish the child – as a deterrent to teach them to behave differently next time, and to signal disapproval, and to some extent to give vent to the angry feelings aroused.

If only punishment actually worked in a predictable manner! We could then go on to discuss the relative ethics of, say, a slap versus a deprivation of television. Unfortunately, all the evidence suggests that punishment of children is not very predictable or specific in its effect. This may lead some parents into an escalation of punishment, with detrimental results.

Punishment then, if it is of sufficient clarity, quantity, speed and logic, and if it is actually applied, rather than threatened, is quite likely to impede the behaviour in progress – even all activity, for a time.

Imagine the young child moving towards the fire with outstretched hand. If it gets a firm slap, it may stop – for a moment. If mother's attention is later distracted, however, it repeats the action, and gets a harder slap, perhaps this time with an angry explanation. Now at this point, the child may have learned something like – "If Mummy sees me going for the fire, she'll slap me so I won't do it," or – "There must be something nasty about fires," or – "There must be something really fascinating about fires," or – "If I really want to get Mum's attention all I have to do is to approach the fire."

Punishment, whether physical or not, sets up all sorts of emotional reverberations in both parent and child. The child may feel guilty and rightly punished, or just as likely, resentful and unfairly punished, say in comparison with its irritating sibling who really started it all. The parent may feel somewhat guilty, especially if they have punished out of proportion to the offence, and yet still feel a need and right to justify the punishment as "deserved" .

Threats, or punishments not actually carried through, are an even less successful form of punishment, although often mentioned by parents who come to the clinic as an example of how they have tried everything and nothing has worked.

A typical example would be as follows: John, Thomas and Susan are always squabbling and are told that if they start up again they will not be allowed to watch any television for the rest of the evening. Soon Susan slyly kicks Thomas, who hits her, and then John shouts at them both to stop it. Mother, trying to make supper and listen to the radio, having had a hard day, loses her temper and imposes the ban. After a slightly shocked pause, the children start to accuse each other. Then John goes to his mother and says he really had nothing to do with the squabble and his favourite programme is coming on so please can he watch it. Mother has by now calmed down a bit and gives in. I expect few would bet on the likelihood of an absence of rows the next night.

DON'T GIVE IN TO ALL DEMANDS

"Love is not enough."
  Bruno Bettelheim

Since the sixties, "old-fashioned" authority has been defied in many spheres. A huge variety of consumer goods is widely available, and as families have become smaller, parents have been able to indulge their children in ways unthought of in previous generations.

This does not always lead to greater happiness, especially for parents who find they have become slaves to demanding and whining children, or that large bribes for good behaviour have only a very temporary effect.

Six-year-old Andrew's parents and grandparents always gave in to his demands. Yet not only was his behaviour dreadful, but his bed-wetting and stealing implied he was insecure. The toddler, Joe, was not just demanding, but also anxious, as his well-meaning father tried to entertain and placate him, while finding it difficult to set any limits.

This can be very puzzling and upsetting, especially for parents who may be convinced that if they had been treated with such kindness as children, they would have been pleased and grateful.

DON'T EXPECT PERFECTION

"Why can't they be like we were – Perfect in every way? Oh, what's the matter with kids today?"
Lionel Bart

I have put this particular expectation on its own, as it is such a key one. It is not that parents openly say they expect their children to be perfect – or even consciously want them to be perfect – and there may indeed be areas where great leeway is allowed. But some areas, for instance school achievement, may be of the greatest importance, and become such a focus for disappointment that strengths of character or skill in other directions may go comparatively unnoticed or unappreciated.

In some ways more fundamental than the idea of the perfect child, is the idea of the perfect parent. After all, children are their parents' responsibility as well as their physical creation, and are a major source of pride and satisfaction – or disappointment – in life. Very often the parents who consult us, both fear that we will blame them for their offspring's inadequacies, and are struggling with this idea themselves. They have often been trying to put right the injustices which they feel they experienced, but find either that the "over-correction" doesn't seem to be working, or that, despite their own efforts, history seems to be repeating itself.

Mrs Williams, for instance, was in this position with her daughter Sarah – desperately concerned to have a good relationship with her, and yet finding that it was not going well.

Winnicott's concept of the "good enough" parent can be a useful educational concept here, as it introduces the idea that not having a "perfect mother" can actually be seen as an advantage to the child. The "perfect parent" does not exist anyway. And perhaps as you realise that your parenting theories are not foolproof, this allows for other possibilities to open up and for you to appreciate unexpected good things about your child.

16

MOVING FORWARD

"What with luck grows into a baby, and becomes
autonomous, biting the hand that feeds it."
  Donald Winnicott

"Children aren't happy with nothing to ignore,
And that's what parents were created for."
  Ogden Nash

Donald Winnicott in earnest, and Ogden Nash more wryly,
are describing the usual phenomena of development, but
instead of telling you how to avoid or bewail the conclusion,
they are describing it as if it were good fortune and the
task of parenthood. And so, how can you begin to think
and feel differently about your irritating child's short-
comings, or at least behave in a way that does not actually
make the problem worse?

IGNORING

The proverbial lesson of the three wise monkeys is: "See

no evil, hear no evil, speak no evil." Parents have usually been told many times that the best thing they can do for a child's annoying behaviour is to ignore it. This can be sound advice, but extremely difficult to follow. If you only ignore a behaviour sometimes, you will be producing what, from a behavioural point of view, is "intermittent partial reinforcement", which makes a behaviour even less likely to disappear.

You will need a plan, and different people will need to adopt different strategies. It will be worth discussing your ideas for ignoring the behaviour with your partner, a friend or relative until you have firmly decided what to do. Maybe even your child has a constructive suggestion. The moment arrives when you feel your irritation rising at the occurrence yet again of the tic, or the untidy bedroom, or the children fighting – whatever it is. Use this as a cue to do something else, preferably enjoyable, to distract yourself. Far be it from me to recommend smoking or drinking, but you may deserve a little reward for not reacting as you normally would. Be creative: pick up your novel, turn up your Walkman, or perhaps you could have a star chart instead of your son. Notice how this becomes easier with practice.

RULES AND REGULATIONS

You may decide that ignoring is not an option, but you have noticed my warnings about punishment. "Penalty" may be a more useful concept. Parking fines are a penalty. We know the rules, we sometimes choose to flout them if our need is great, and if we are caught, well, the payment of a fine is not a public disgrace, but may make us think twice about doing it the next time in the same place. Not very much emotion is usually expended.

Children, too, could have small fixed penalties for infringement of household rules. This works quite well on a short-term basis for minor problems, a penny off pocket money for clothes left on the floor for instance, or a one-off grounding for coming in late. Penalties ideally should be known in advance, and they should be fairly rare. They should be logical and their purpose understood by the child – for instance a tidy house, or parents being assured of their safety. They are best applied dispassionately, so that anger and insult are not added. The longer-term goal is that the child takes on their own responsibility for behaving considerately to others.

LOOK OUT FOR WHAT YOU ARE HOPING FOR

The usual simple, but excellent, advice is to praise or reward good behaviour – but in the first place you have to be in the frame of mind to notice it.

A slight reduction, or even an absence, of trouble can go unobserved, so your first task is to be on the alert for even a slight improvement so that you can comment favourably.

What would be an improvement? Have you told your child what you would like to see in a positive way? Star charts are often successfully used with young children for little everyday improvements, and have the advantage that they are clear and systematic, and can be looked at with joint pride by parent and child.

NOTICE WHAT WORKS

Just possibly, your teenage child has entered the stage when a favourable comment about their appearance will instantly cause them to swear never to comb their hair again – or whatever the issue is. Be more canny. Notice which of your responses meets with more success. If, as is not uncommon, you have unintentionally trained your child to ignore you, you may have to enlarge your repertoire of responses to get any effect. Just shouting louder will not be helpful, as you want to maintain a good relationship, but occasional moments of humorous melodrama may serve as a reminder that mothers and fathers have feelings too.

RE-THINK YOUR IDEAS

Your child may have received a terrible school report, but try and avoid catastrophising ("He'll end up on the streets!"), blaming him, yourself or the school. It is possible, by predicting future difficulties, to create self-fulfilling prophecies.

The opposite way round is more interesting. Given that your child is irritable and bad-tempered, or perhaps is academically weak, how much is it possible to improve the outcome by your own and others' efforts? How much is it sensible to accept and make the best of the situation?

LOOK AT YOUR UNDERLYING BELIEFS ABOUT THE SITUATION

Which of these are your own ideas, and what is the source of them? For instance, there might be a strong family tradition that there is always one difficult child in every family, and nothing can be done about it. Or you may have picked up the idea from school that every misdemeanour, however small, must be punished. Or you may believe that one particular child should never be denied what he wants, as he has had a difficult start in life. It may be worthwhile arguing with yourself if you realise that some of these ideas are too absolute to be useful.

IDENTIFY THE ACCOMPANYING EMOTIONS

You could think about a particular incident. Your son started university but he left in the middle of his second term. He doesn't want to discuss why, but is just lying around at home, apparently in training to become a couch potato.

If this is the first time anything like this has happened you may feel upset and disappointed, a little bit angry, quite possibly ashamed when you think of your sister's children who are all doing sickeningly well. You probably feel concerned about what might have happened to your son. If you are of an imaginative and "catastrophising" turn of mind you may be thinking of schizophrenia or drugs, and be feeling helpless, despairing and uncertain.

As in the example above, you may come across emotions which you yourself realise are so out of proportion that they must be related to other ideas, not only to the situation at hand.

Perhaps this event connects up with previous similar incidents which this particular child was involved in. For instance, he once threw in a part-time job because he was irritated by some of the people there. Your mind is running on themes of ... he will never stick at anything ... he will never get a job ... I shall be disgraced in front of everyone and there will be nobody to look after me in my old age ... and so on.

Or, start with that feeling of disappointment. When have you felt like this before? This time what may come to mind may not be connected with your son, but with someone else. Your best friend cancelled a long-standing arrangement with you last week. How did you respond? How do you characteristically respond? Looking back, does your childhood seem to have been full of disappointments? Were your parents chronically dissatisfied with their life, and perhaps your own contribution?

This train of thought may show you that your current emotional response has little to do with the immediate current situation.

CONSIDER YOUR PAST SUCCESSES

Just as you are beginning to think you are a hopeless case, doomed by negativity in your past experience, spend a while considering how you have been successful in overcoming feelings of disappointment in the past. Some of these may have happened accidentally, but you can learn from them. Suppose you did not get into the university of your first choice, but when you compared notes with your best friend you discovered you were both going to the same place, which in the end you greatly enjoyed.

One of the things you did right here was to share the news of your disappointment with someone else, whether or not you let them know how bad you felt about it. This allowed you to check the validity of your emotional response. And you need to have the sort of confidantes who do not immediately leap to criticise you as soon as they feel you are vulnerable.

Which relative, friend or colleague was the most helpful when you last had a bit of bad news? How many people do you know who are likely to be in a similar position and therefore not judgemental?

LOOK FOR THE POSITIVE

Returning to your son the couch potato: can this be viewed in a positive light? At least he is behaving independently, and not slavishly following his parents' received ideas. You know where he is, and already he is better qualified than John Major. Perhaps he is revolting against the materialism of the world, or perhaps he just needs a rest.

Don't blind yourself to the negative features of your son's behaviour, but be aware of the range of possibilities. It is unfortunately a human trait to perceive the negative rather than the positive. In interpersonal relationships this may lead to a vicious circle.

LOOK FORWARD

Parenthood is a gamble, but one in which the majority gain great rewards, even if they do not realise it until they become grandparents. The wonderful thing about children is that they are always developing and becoming new people, so there is no need to become stuck in the hopelessness of the present. You can expect too much of your children, and they may fail to live up to your expectations. You may expect to be a perfect parent and be disappointed in yourself. Despite all of this, you care for your children and they care for you. So, I would advise you to keep your expectations moderate but your hopes high, agreeing with Samuel Johnson that:

"Hope is itself a species of happiness, and perhaps, the chief happiness which this world affords."

INDEX

SELECTED BIBLIOGRAPHY

Aries, Philippe (translated by Robert Baldick).
Centuries of Childhood. A Social History of Family Life
(Jonathan Cape, 1962)

Beck, Aaron.
Cognitive Therapy and the Emotional Disorders
(International Universities Press, 1976)

Bowlby, John
Attachment and Loss
(Hogarth Press, 1969)

Carroll, Lewis
Alice's Adventures in Wonderland
(Macmillan and Co, 1896)

Chess, Stella and Thomas, Alexander
Origins and Evolution of Behavior Disorders
(Brunner/Mazel, 1984)

Festinger, Leo
A Theory of Cognitive Dissonance
(Harper and Row, 1957)

Ellis, Albert and Grieger, Russell (eds)
Handbook of Rational-Emotive Therapy
(Springer Publishing Company, 1977)

Fodor, Nandor and Gaynor, Frank
Freud. Dictionary of Psychoanalysis
(The Philosophical Library Inc. 1950)

Johnson, Wendell
People in Quandaries
(Harper and Brothers, 1946)

Klaus, Marshall H and Kennell, John H
Parent-Infant Bonding
(Second edition, CV Mosby Company, 1982)

Leff, Julian and Vaughan, Christine
Expressed Emotions in Families
(Guildford Press, 1985)

McKey, RH et al
The Impace of Head Start on Children, Families and Communities
(CSR, 1985)

Patterson, GR
Coercive Family Process
(Castalia, 1982)

Pincus, Lily
Death and the Family
(Faber and Faber, 1976)

Raphael, Beverley
The Anatomy of Bereavement
(Hutchinson and Co, 1984)

Renvoize, Jean
Children in Danger
(Routledge and Kegan Paul, 1974)

Rutter, Micchael et al
Fifteen Thousand Hours: Secondary Schools and their Effects on Children
Open Books, 1979

Seligman, Martin EP
Learned Optimism
Alfred A Knopf, 1991

Spitz, Rene
The First Yearo f Life
(International Universities Press Ltd., 1965)

Spock, Benjamin
Baby and Child Care
(Pocket Books Inc, 1957)

Tatar, Maria
The Hard Facts of the Grimms' Fairy Tales
(Princeton University Press, 1987)

Winicott, DW
The Child, the Family and the Outside World
(Penguin Books, 1964)

Just published:

PROBLEM PERIODS
  Causes, Symptoms and Relief
Dr Caroline Shreeve

Few women can escape problems with their period. This book examines the whole spectrum of menstrual problems that can arise between the first period and menopause.

Coming soon:

CHILDCARE
  A Guide for the Working Parent
Geraldine Bown

Childcare is the cause of endless concern for working parents, whatever the age of their child or children. And it's the one area where a parent can't afford to make a mistake; this comprehensive book should ensure that you don't.